CHARLES DRAZIN *on*

Blue Velvet

Bloomsbury Movie Guides

CHARLES DRAZIN *on*

Blue Velvet

Bloomsbury Movie Guide No.3

BLOOMSBURY

Published by Bloomsbury Publishing, New York and London.
Distributed to the trade by St. Martin's Press

A CIP catalogue record for this book
is available from the Library of Congress

ISBN 1-58234-029-3

First published in Great Britain in 1998 by Bloomsbury Publishing Plc.

First U.S. Edition 1999
10 9 8 7 6 5 4 3 2 1

Typeset by Palimpsest Book Production Limited,
Polmont, Stirlingshire
Printed in Great Britain by
Clays Ltd, St Ives plc

A

alter ego

See **duality, double identity and doubles**.

America

America is a pretty peculiar place. Perhaps you have to be an outsider to appreciate this. It seems to me that if David Lynch's vision of an American town is an outlandish one, it is so because he has retained the ability of a child, or a stranger, to be surprised by his surroundings. He sees and feels things with the intensity of someone experiencing these things for the first time.

What makes America seem even more peculiar to the outsider is its very familiarity. We share the same language, we see images of it all the time on the TV or at the cinema, we're surrounded by its products. So it's a shock to visit and to find a place more alien than anywhere you've been before. It's this strangeness in the normal that *Blue Velvet* is so attuned to.

A few years ago I went to America for the first time. I visited my uncle, who lives in a small town in Indiana that I had never heard of before. I got off a train that stopped in Main Street. Plonked down in this alien but familiar place, the simplest things demanded a conscious appraisal. The primary **colours**. The canary-yellow school buses, the shiny blue vans of the US Mail, the deep red McDonalds' sign in the shopping mall. Everything seemed big but friendly. It was the sort of place where the firemen would wave as their trucks went by.

What accounted for this cosiness? Perhaps the isolating vastness of the land – the realisation that you'd have to travel miles and miles to get to the next town. It meant that each individual town felt more like a self-contained community. In Britain, where towns sprawl into each other and everywhere is just a short journey away from everywhere else, our sense of township is imprecise. *Blue Velvet*'s 'Welcome to **Lumberton**' billboard seems like a meaningful civic gesture; 'Welcome to Watford' would seem pointless because it would be so hard to figure out when exactly you'd left Northwood or Ruislip or whatever other place it becomes.

In those American towns you're under no illusion that you've arrived in a different place, yet the various faces they present to you as a visitor are so borrowed from somewhere else that you feel like you're in a nowhereland. My uncle took me out to dinner at Bruno's Swiss Inn. There seemed to be nothing Swiss about our meal at all, and it was hard to imagine anywhere less like Switzerland than the flat landscape of Indiana. We ate our large, bland pizzas, and dipped our breadsticks in a cheese sauce that tasted of sugar. As I walked to the car afterwards, I felt full but still vaguely dissatisfied. I looked wistfully up the road to the other restaurants in their identical chalets and with their large display boards on gaudily decorated stilts receding into infinity. 'FOR A HEART HEALTHY MENU & 21 ENTREES UNDER TEN DOLLARS DINE AT SORRENTO' read the one nearest us, the name SORRENTO written in flame-red letters spewed forth from a volcano.

As I imagined the twenty-one different cheese dips all tasting of sugar, the full horror of the illusory variety sank in. It's easy to see why the Americans love the movies. In a land without roots where everything has been put together from scratch, pretence and make-believe become second nature. If you look at a map of America the states look like flapjacks cut up in a baking tray. There's nothing to distinguish the one from the other; they don't seem to follow any natural boundaries. There's something askew in the way these imaginary lines carve up the void. The scale of possible boredom in a country like this is daunting.

Its very vastness is mirrored within the towns. The whole notion of 'small-town America' can seem rather absurd because the area these towns actually cover is huge. One afternoon I went for a walk in the neighbourhood, past large, comfortable-looking clapboard houses each with its expanse of lawn. Eventually I realised that I was lost. I wasn't worried because I thought that sooner or later I'd get to a main road and be able to ask directions – like in a normal place. But I walked on and on, and there seemed no sign of the avenue I had turned into ever ending, and – as the house numbers were running in the high four figures – no reason why it ever should. I tried to use my homing instinct, taking what seemed to be the most likely turns. Invariably successful in London, this method was useless here. The place confounded any sense of direction – the neighbourhood was just too much alike. I had the impression that home could have been a few yards away or miles away. Here was the size and sameness of America. As I began to despair of ever getting home, but passed the ninety-ninth house that looked just like home – with the pick-up truck in the drive and the practice basketball net over the garage – I began to understand why some residents might want to escape over a rainbow if they could.

I'd been there only two days but already felt like screaming. I wondered how people could spend their whole lives there. It seemed to me to require a kind of sleepwalking. In a town where there was endless choice but the best place to eat was Bruno's Swiss Inn it didn't do to think too much. If you did, sooner or later you'd go mad. My uncle was already showing the signs. We drove miles and miles to find the supermarket that sold the cheapest bananas. In his top pocket he kept a little notebook in which he wrote down the prices of everything he bought in the course of the day. He put the lists in a kitchen drawer, where they piled up forgotten. In such a place the thoughtful have to cultivate such eccentricity, do drugs or dream.

The monotony and order of the town seemed to demand a counterbalance, so that its continuing calm seemed sinister. Such a place, I thought, would breed powerful fantasies as surely as the endless prairie land around it bred tornados. You could see how easily it could produce both a Jeffrey and a Frank, and you could imagine how lost a stranger like Dorothy might feel.

I was thankful to get back on the train to Chicago and leave the town behind, a little island in the vast plain of Middle America. A day later a tornado ripped through the place and killed two people.

See **Zippergate**.

'Angriest Dog in the World, The'

Frank Booth, so often a victim of his own helpless rage, often reminds me of the angriest dog in the world. Over a period of nine years from 1983 David Lynch drew a cartoon for the *LA Reader* about this poor creature. Every issue the captions would change, but the picture of the dog would remain the same – 'The dog who is so angry he cannot move. He cannot sleep. He can just barely gowl. Bound so tightly with tension and anger, he approaches the state of rigor mortis.' In the last frame it's night-time and the angriest dog is still growling. Straining at his leash, he looks as much like a shark or a crocodile as a dog. The big difference is that in Frank's case the leash has snapped; he's away, savaging people.

Arlene's

The diner in which Jeffrey persuades Sandy to help him with his plan to get into Dorothy's apartment. He meets her here on another occasion to tell her what he's discovered about **Frank**, and it's here that he kisses her for the first time.

Aunt Barbara

'Jeffrey, you're not going down by Lincoln, are you?' asks Aunt Barbara, when Jeffrey goes out for a walk after dark. Lincoln Street is the rough part of town, it's where **Deep River Apartments** is, and Aunt Barbara's inquiry amounts to a warning to stay away. In the absence of his father it is the only parental advice Jeffrey ever receives in the Beaumont household.

But Aunt Barbara is easily ignored as the over-cautious grown-up. Not only would she never stray into a bad neighbourhood, but she would never talk to strangers, never go out after dark, and probably she doesn't smoke or drink. Her life is the abnegation of unpredictable experience, a denial of the upsetting or the unpleasant. Perhaps this is why she has remained a maiden aunt.

In some way she *hasn't* grown up – hasn't ventured beyond the protective wall of childhood innocence that is part of growing up. 'I don't see how they do it,' she says as she looks at a **robin** with an insect in its beak. 'I could never eat a bug.' And perhaps she would find the blood of lost virginity equally appalling.

Aunt Barbara's world is the drawing-room and the breakfast table. If she knew what Jeffrey had been up to, smelling salts would be required to revive her. Aunt Barbara is endearing but infuriating. She lives in a world of reassuring certainty and stifling conformity. The trouble with Aunt Barbaras – and most of us know one – is that you just can't get through to them. There is a gulf in understanding that can never be bridged. Sometimes it's called the generation gap, but it's as much an experience gap. Aunt Barbara is one of those adults who suffer from the delusion that because they're older they must therefore be wiser too.

'Sometimes it helps to talk things over,' she says when Jeffrey comes down to the breakfast table with a black eye. Jeffrey knows it's no use. 'Aunt Barbara. I love you, but you're gonna get it . . .'

By the time Aunt Barbara made her appearance in the final film she had undergone a process of normalisation. In the script she displays the kind of eccentricity that Lynch would indulge a taste for with the characters of *Twin Peaks*. This earlier Aunt Barabara has a strange fascination with termites – which is at odds with the squeamish spinster of the film who blanches at the sight of a bug. She tells Jeffrey one evening that she's seen some of the creatures in the house. When Jeffrey – who is about to go off to have dinner with the Williams family – leaves the room, she starts to hunt for them. She taps the walls and a termite falls down on to the carpet. She picks it up and looks at it closely. Jeffrey returns home late at night to discover this note together with two dead termites: 'JEFFREY, HONEY, I FOUND THESE. LOVE, AUNT BARBARA.'

The removal of the episode made her seem more timorous than mad, allowing the Beaumont family to represent a veneer of normality.

B

Bacon, Francis (1909–1992)

'Francis Bacon is, to me, the main guy, the number one kinda
hero painter,' Lynch has said. He saw Bacon's exhibition at the
Marlborough-Gerson Gallery in New York in 1968, soon after he
had first begun to experiment with film at art school, 'and it was
really one of the most powerful things I ever saw in my life'. In *Blue
Velvet* the traces of Lynch's hero can be found in the depiction of the
self-destructive Dorothy in her apartment. Exposed and vulnerable
against the slabs of bare wall and carpet, which are in **colours** that
belong more to a slaughterhouse than a home, she brings to mind
Henrietta Moraes (Lying Figure with Hypodermic Syringe), 1963. She
brings to mind several Bacon paintings, actually. The two artists are
one in their sense of humanity's violent contradiction.

I was interested to read an introduction to a recent book of Bacon's
portraits by the Czech writer Milan Kundera. He wrote that looking at
a Bacon portrait-triptych reminded him of an incident long ago when
he was living in Prague under the communists. A young woman friend
of his had been interrogated by the police about his activities. They
met to get their stories straight just in case he was interrogated too. She
was intelligent and spirited, and possessed a formidable self-control,
Kundera remembered, but, 'suddenly, fear like a great knife had laid
her open. She was gaping wide before me like the split carcass of a
heifer hanging from a meat hook.'

Several times during their meeting Kundera's friend excused herself
to go to the toilet.

The noise of the water refilling the tank practically never let
up, and I suddenly had the urge to rape her. I know what
I'm saying. Rape her, not make love to her. I didn't want
tenderness from her. I wanted to bring my hand brutally on
her face and in one swift instant take her completely, with all her
unbearably arousing contradictions: with her impeccable outfit
along with her rebellious guts, her good sense along with her
fear, her pride along with her misery. I sensed that all those
contradictions harboured her essence, that treasure, that nugget
of gold, that diamond hidden in the depths.

This 'uncalled for and unconscionable desire' that Kundera writes
of can be found as much in *Blue Velvet* as in Bacon's paintings.
Both Jeffrey and Frank are prey to a similar kind of perversity,
just as Dorothy is a similar kind of victim. By one of those odd
coincidences, I've come to know very well the person who modelled for the Bacon tryptich that Kundera was writing about. I
can verify that she is the mixture of contradictions that Bacon
painted.

See **influences**.

Badalamenti, Angelo (b. 1937)

He's two people in *Blue Velvet*: Andy Badale, the man who was hired
as a singing coach to Isabella Rossellini and makes an appearance
as the piano player in **the Slow Club**; and Angelo Badalamenti,
who, although it had not been originally intended, would write
the score for the film and go on to become one of the most
successful film composers of recent times. He had worked as a

junior high school teacher in Brooklyn and was little known before
his collaboration with David Lynch. Indeed, several filmographies
assume that *Blue Velvet* was Badalamenti's first film score. In a way
it was. In the previous decade he contributed songs to *Gordon's
War* and *Across the Great Divide*, and wrote the score for Ivan
Passer's film *Law and Disorder*, but in each case was credited as
Andy Badale.

When it came to *Blue Velvet*, no doubt encouraged by the other
extravagant Italian names on the production – De Laurentiis, Rossellini
– and given a role where he was encouraged to be extravagant too, for
the first time he used his full name: Angelo Badalamenti.

There was something fated about his coming together with David
Lynch – and the fact that they were introduced by a man called,
of all names, Caruso, encourages one to view their partnership in a
providential light. In *Blue Velvet* there's a seamless blend of music
and picture – they bring each other out. If such close collaborations
tend to involve the most visual of directors – one thinks of Herrman
and Hitchcock, Morricone and Leone – then perhaps it's because
the essence of cinema, in the rhythm and flow of its images, is a
musical one.

Since *Blue Velvet* Badalamenti has worked on all Lynch's movies.
Badalamenti's own characterisation of his **music** as 'tragically dark'
suggests their shared sensibility, and it was natural that, just as Lynch
pulled Badalamenti into his movie world, so Badalamenti should have
pulled Lynch into his musical world. In 1989 the two co-produced
an album for Julee Cruise, *Floating into the Night*; Badalamenti wrote
the music and Lynch wrote the lyrics. They also co-wrote and
co-produced *Industrial Symphony No. 1*, a filmed performance at the
Brooklyn Academy of Music, featuring Laura Dern, Nicolas Cage and
Julee Cruise.

Badalamenti was born in Brooklyn to an Italian father and an
American mother. He studied at the Eastman School of Music in

Rochester and the Manhattan School of Music, where he received master's degrees in composition, French horn and piano. Other films include *Tough Guys Don't Dance*; *A Nightmare on Elm Street III: Dream Warriors*; *Cousins*; *Wild at Heart*; *The Comfort of Strangers*; *Twin Peaks: Fire Walk With Me*; *La Cité des enfants perdus*, for which he received a César nomination; and *Lost Highway*. He won a Grammy for the music in the *Twin Peaks* TV series.

Beaumont, Jeffrey

See **Jeffrey**

Beaumont, Mr

When Jeffrey visits his father in hospital Mr Beaumont tries desperately hard to speak to him but finds it impossible. He just gurgles a bit. Had he been able to talk, one feels it would probably have been to issue some terrible warning. This sense of him as a stricken guardian not being there to protect his son is brought out by a dream Jeffrey has after he witnesses Frank brutalise Dorothy in **Deep River Apartments**. He sees Dorothy begging to be hit and Frank roaring bestially, but the first image of this nightmare is his father in hospital mouthing words distorted beyond certain comprehension. In his helplessness there's a feeling of the baton being passed over to the next generation. As the son begins to exercise the independence of adulthood, the father, trapped in a hospital bed, becomes like a **child** in need of help.

In the script Mr Beaumont did say a few words to his visiting son. 'Hi, Jeff' and 'Good to see you, son.' But the scene as it is finally shot rendered him silent and becomes much more powerful as a tableau of stricken non-communication.

★   ★   ★

Beaumont, Mrs

She's watching TV when her husband has his seizure and she's watching TV when Jeffrey ventures out at night to begin his quest into the mystery of the severed **ear**. Aunt Barbara checks with her nephew that he's not going anywhere near Lincoln, the bad part of town. But Mrs Beaumont's only concern is to ask Jeffrey whether he wants to borrow the car. She seems somehow immunised from real life by the air waves. She is a couch potato indulging in a soft-core **voyeurism** while her son goes out after the hard stuff.

But walk down any residential street during prime-time hours, see the blue glow emanating from virtually every sitting-room window, and you'll appreciate that she is just one of the silent majority too enwrapped in the soap or the thriller or the film of the day to murmur a word. It is life disarmed and safely imprisoned behind the TV screen.

Mrs Beaumont has reached the age where her battles are behind her. She has opted for middle-class seclusion. Like Mrs Williams, she is a quiet, stay-at-home wife, belonging to an earlier generation. These are the sort of mothers David Lynch would have known when he was growing up in **the fifties**. If the delineation of Mrs Beaumont as a character is shadowy, it's in accordance with the young person's viewpoint of the film. In her very blandness she captures the truth that to teenagers all parents look and behave alike.

Lynch's original conception of Mrs Beaumont was much more naturalistic but contrary to the final **mood** and focus of the film. In the script she is a worried wife and an interventionist mother. Her stress is such that the **family** doctor comes round one evening to administer tranquillisers. The pressures which she must be under but which we don't see in the finished film are much more obvious. It's Mrs Beaumont who after her husband's stroke summons Jeffrey home from college, telling him that he must work in the family store, as now they won't be able to afford to pay for his education. She also tells him when to go and see his father, and tells him off when he comes home late. 'You can't just stay out half the night and carry on, Jeffrey. There's got to be some order.'

Most 20-year-olds will recognise this Mrs Beaumont. She's exasperatingly true to life. By the time she reached the screen the TV had taken the place of her tranquillisers and she was effectively muzzled. Lost in her soap-opera limbo, and with Mr Beaumont stricken in hospital, there's a sense of Jeffrey having to find his way on his own for the first time.

Ben

Ben runs a brothel which is next to a bar called **This is It**. He also looks after the money side of Frank's **drugs** business. When the **gang** drops by with Dorothy and their hostage, Jeffrey, it's more than just a social visit. It's also an occasion for Frank to pick up a wad of notes.

Ben is **Lumberton**'s king – or queen – of fopdom. His green paisley jacket and frilled shirt with flounced sleeves set off nicely his painted face and rouged lips. In one limp-wristed hand, inexplicably bandaged, he flourishes a cigarette holder. He's so outlandish that it's a struggle to describe him. Frank calls him 'suave', and perhaps this comes closest to capturing his showbiz glamour. 'You're so fucking suave!' he exclaims admiringly, and 'We love Ben!' Camp but deadly, Ben's the one person Frank looks up to.

Ben's every bit as violent as Frank. The only real difference is that he enjoys it so much more. There's something desperate about Frank's violence. He can scarcely control himself. But Ben is a connoisseur, used to lingering over his pleasures. When Frank slugs his frightened hostage for not being polite enough, the men in his gang laugh hard but nervously – they know too well how easy it is for him to spin out of control. Only Ben seems truly relaxed.

It's as if he's looking down from some high summit, like a

Mephistophelian deity to whom Frank and his gang pay court. As Jeffrey is held for Ben to punch him in the stomach with unhurried calm, he's the plaything that the underlings have procured for their master's amusement.

In as much as Frank could wish to change himself, probably he'd want to be more like Ben, to take life more easily and to enjoy his cruelty instead of always being so het up about everything. He would also be drawn to the domesticity of Ben's life, so much does he seem to hanker after **family** routine himself. With matronly fat ladies in attendance, it is Ben's place that provides the nearest thing to a home for the gang, and it is here that Dorothy's kidnapped son and husband are kept hostage.

Ben is calculating where Frank is spontaneous, and in their criminal enterprise together it's really Ben who pulls the strings. He controls Frank with the pills he pops into his mouth, the money he pays for services rendered, and his coolness that Frank so admires. Of the two he is by far the more evil, for he can help himself.

See **Stockwell, Dean**.

black-and-colour

I always think of *Blue Velvet* as a black-and-colour film. Lynch's instinct for the contrast of black and white, in which he had made both *Eraserhead* and *The Elephant Man*, caused him at first to experiment with desaturated **colours**. When this did not work, he and cinematographer **Frederick Elmes** decided to go to the other extreme, using supersaturated colours, but it is blackness which brings out their contrast. It's like a wash on the canvas, fixing and giving an edge to the other values. It also adds **mood** and mystery. Talking of his **painting**, Lynch has commented:

If you have some shadow or **darkness** in the frame, then your mind can travel in there and dream. In general, colour is a little too real. It's too close. It doesn't make you dream much. If everything is visible, and there's too much light, the thing is what it is, but it isn't any more than that.

Blue Lady, the

Dorothy's nightclub name, appropriate not only because she sings 'Blue Velvet', but also because she's sad and sexy.

See **colours**.

blue velvet

As Frank watches Dorothy sing for him in **the Slow Club** he kneads a piece of blue velvet. He has cut it from her blue gown, which represents everything he most needs. He forces her to wear it when he visits her at **Deep River Apartments**. When she stuffs its cord into his mouth, he's like a baby suckling on his mother's breast. 'Baby wants blue velvet!' He in turn stuffs it into her mouth and vagina. It's an act of violation but also of further regression. As the blue velvet makes an umbilical **connection**, it's as if he wants to climb back into the womb. It's sign too of his impotence, the blue velvet standing in for the sexual act he cannot properly perform himself. The blue velvet makes him feel strong and secure. It becomes a fetish object. It's the charm with which he blesses all his activities, the symbol of his diseased love, in which **sex** and destruction are indistinguishable. If Frank associates the blue velvet with many, often contradictory things, perhaps finally it stands best as a symbol for inexplicable, ever-shifting infatuation.

On the soundtrack album of *Blue Velvet* you can hear Isabella Rossellini sing the title song, but not Bobby Vinton, whose version accompanies the opening and closing scenes of the film. This is like buying *Evita* to find the one song missing is 'Don't Cry for Me, Argentina'. 'Copyright problems,' replied the record company when I wrote to inquire. But on the strength of the movie, Bobby Vinton himself made a comeback. For two weeks in October 1990 'Blue Velvet' was at the top of the UK singles charts. It was like the blue skies returning.

If you visit Branson, Missouri – a sort of Las Vegas of the Deep South – you can hear Vinton sing the song six nights a week in his own 'Blue Velvet Theatre'. Descriptions of the enterprise suggest a crusade to cement the song's original innocence. It's a place where **families** are encouraged to come, and where, doubtless, all mention of Frank and Dorothy is discouraged.

The slippery, transient nature of blue velvet, sliding between purity and defilement. An advertisement on TV: a floating blue ribbon gently drapes itself over a beautiful girl's eyes. An easy-listening voice croons, 'She wore blue velvet . . .', and the slogan 'Experience the touch' greets the apparition of a four-pack of Kleenex Double Velvet toilet paper.

Blue Velvet

The first time I saw *Blue Velvet* was at the Screen on Baker Street. With hindsight this was appropriate, as that great **voyeur** Sherlock Holmes lived only a few doors up the road. It was in a small auditorium, which in the **darkness** seemed not much larger than Dorothy's **closet**, and I felt like Jeffrey spying through the slats of the closet's louvred door – a feeling that the film's letterbox format only encouraged. Of all films, *Blue Velvet* is a peculiarly private pleasure – if that is the right word – best enjoyed, or endured, in **secret**.

The cinema is the only place in which the film can be properly appreciated, for even in the film's proper format the electronic blur of the TV screen renders the **colours** and spatial dimensions untrue. Yet before an audience its intense feeling can be trivialised, as they laugh during the most disturbing moments, resisting rather than yielding to the **mood**. (But then perhaps this is partly what *Blue Velvet* is about – how frightened people are to face their feelings.)

What are the perfect conditions for seeing *Blue Velvet*? I think the auditorium must be so dark that you don't even know that anybody else is there, and the audience so silent that they seem to be in a trance or some shocked stupor.

And you have to be alone. Most of all, you have to be alone. I went to see it with my then girlfriend. I remember us trailing out of the auditorium in awkward silence. She looked as if she had been hit, and treated my attempts to defend the film as a kind of aggravated assault. We argued about it over a bad-tempered meal, then went home in sulky silence.

If it took a day or two for our frostiness to subside. We were lucky. A friend recently told me that he knew of a marriage that had ended in divorce over the film.

Booth, Frank

See **Frank**.

Bosch, Hieronymous (c. 1460–1516)

See **influences; paradise lost; Rockwell, Norman**.

C

Central

The high school in **Lumberton** where Sandy is a senior. Jeffrey used to go there too. Both think it a dull place.

children

At the beginning of the film, after the fire engine has gone by, we see seven children escorted over the road by a crossing attendant. There is a large gap between the third and the fourth child. I imagine Dorothy's Donny, had he not been kidnapped, filling the space. The final image of the film, in which we see him restored to his mother, provides a counterpoint. These children, so closely guarded, with that gap where Donny might have been, suggest humanity's terrible frailty. A few seconds later a middle-aged man collapses unexpectedly in the tranquillity of his own garden.

chipped tooth

A shocking, defining image of Dorothy is her smile of ecstasy after Jeffrey has hit her. A chip in her tooth seems to catch and fragment the light like a diamond. The tooth was broken when Isabella Rossellini's brother threw a telephone at her in a childhood argument. When she began modelling, Lancôme used undertakers' wax to fill in the crack.

closet, the

The role of the closet as a place of sexual **secrets** is time-honoured, standard accoutrement of farce and – it seems in the age of **Zippergate** – public life. While having **sex** in the cupboard of a Washington hotel President Kennedy spoke of one of his predecessors, who performed it in a coat cupboard outside the Oval Office.

In the origin of the phrase 'skeleton in the cupboard' can be found a tale with all the sexual violence and kinkiness depicted in *Blue Velvet.* To quote from *Brewer's Dictionary of Phrase and Fable*:

> The story is that someone without a single care or trouble in the world had to be found. After a long and unsuccessful search a lady was discovered who all thought would 'fill the bill'; but to the great surprise of the inquirers, after she had satisfied them on all points and the quest seemed to be achieved, she took them upstairs and there opened a closet which contained a human skeleton. 'I try', said she, 'to keep my trouble to myself, but every night my husband compels me to kiss that skeleton.' She then explained that the skeleton was once her husband's rival, killed in a duel.

But long before Jeffrey sneaked into Dorothy's a cupboard was a place of discovery. One thinks of the children in *The Lion, the Witch and the Wardrobe*, pushing their way through the coats into the magic land of Narnia. As in dreams, sometimes you have to go to a dark place to discover a new world.

collaborators

It is one of the hallmarks of the film-maker with a personal vision that he should gather about himself a family of people in tune with his approach. Although Lynch has had favourite actors like Jack Nance and Kyle MacLachlan, this continuity is perhaps most evident among those who have worked regularly with him behind the camera, such as **Angelo Badalamenti (music)**, **Frederick Elmes** (cinematography), **Patricia Norris (costume** and production design) and **Alan Splet (sound** design).

The contributions of these collaborators are distinctive, but function within the ambience that Lynch has created. Lynch's working method accounts for a sense in *Blue Velvet* of infinite possibility. He responds to the material rather than attempts to force it into a preconceived framework. The result is something organic that has its own independent life. Lynch once described his approach to **painting** as being 'like the Japanese with the garden'. The same, I think, is true of his attitude to his collaborators: 'Nature is doing all this stuff, and all they do is maybe take a branch and trim it, impose their will on it, and make it grow a certain way. And they prune, and they keep certain things out. But the plants are doing most of the work. It's a two-way street – nature and man working together.'

colours

The beginning of *Blue Velvet* is like an art lesson. We are introduced to the palette of primary colours: the blue of the sky, the yellow of the tulips, the red of the roses. With these colours all other colours can be made.

No colour alone is good or bad, although each may carry with it certain associations. Blue evokes sadness and sexuality, as red does danger and violation. So there's the blood-red lipstick that Frank smears over Jeffrey's face just before he beats him up in **Meadow Lane**. And when later he tries to kill him, an act which he finds as much **sexual** as destructive, he wears a red shirt and clutches Dorothy's blue gown.

It's the unbalanced people in *Blue Velvet* who wear primary colours in isolation. So the police traitor Detective Gordon is **the Yellow**

Man, and Dorothy is **the Blue Lady**. She dresses in red and blue – red shoes and blue velvet gown, red lipstick and blue eye shadow. When she sings at **the Slow Club** she's bathed in red and blue light. Deeply disturbed, it's not so much that she has a screw loose as that she needs a little bit of yellow. We never see her in the daytime until the very last scene in the film, when a sober brown blouse suggests a new-found equilibrium. Little Donny is with her. He wears red, blue and yellow – a complete set of primary colours with which to start out in life.

And just before, at the Beaumonts' house, as the first **robin** arrives, the characters are dressed in combinations of white – the purest colour, the colour that contains all the other colours of the spectrum.

See **costume drama**.

comedy

Whenever there's a dog around, you can be pretty sure something funny will happen sooner or later. And somehow, when in the opening seconds of the film you see a Dalmatian sitting on the running board of a red fire engine, you know that, whatever else *Blue Velvet* may be, it's a comedy too.

When Mr Beaumont has his seizure and collapses to the ground with his spurting hose, a dog is quickly on the scene. But instead of bounding off like Lassie to fetch an ambulance, it barks and bites excitedly at the jet of water, leaving Mr Beaumont to his fate. Lynch would rework the macabre humour of this scene in *Wild at Heart*. After a bank raid we see two blood-bespattered tellers. One of them has had his hand shot off. 'They sew them things back on,' his colleague tells him. 'Work as good as new.' They grope around on the floor looking for the missing hand. 'Gotta be here somewhere,' we hear one of them say, as the film cuts to a dog trotting cheerfully out of the front entrance with the hand in his mouth.

Dogs are great comic material because they remain resolutely themselves in defiance of convention. Both these scenes are funny, but they also capture a truth about life – that it goes on, indifferent to our personal tragedies.

The comic set piece of the film is Ben's place. Ben is effeminate, yet at the same time he holds a patriarchal sway over his little kingdom. Fat matronly ladies dance attendance on him, 'You're so suave!' says Frank, impressed. The humour lies in the scene's perverse respectability. You don't expect hardened criminals to be quite so homely.

Yet it's a mysterious, unsettling humour. You don't know which way it will turn. What's so powerful about this scene is the way the absurd slides so quickly into pathos. As Ben mimes the words of an old Roy Orbison song, Dorothy emerges from a back room in a daze, rejected by her son.

The conventional drama proceeds by means of a series of scenes of fixed emotional value. High drama is followed by a love scene or one of comic relief. But in *Blue Velvet* the love scene could be a torture scene and a comic scene as well.

In this intermingling of moods Lynch gets closer than just about any other contemporary film-maker to the way human beings actually *feel*. We may present a consistent front to the world, but we oscillate between different emotions: 'I didn't know whether to laugh or cry.'

connections

Alfred Hitchcock used to speak of 'pure cinema', Michael Powell of the 'composed film'. While most movies are, as Hitchcock put it, just 'photographs of people talking', in pure cinema 'every piece of film that you put in the picture should have a purpose. You cannot put it together indiscriminately. It's like notes of **music**. They must make their point.' *Blue Velvet* is one of those very few films – as rare as four-leaf clovers – that makes full use of its medium, achieving the integration of all the elements that it encompasses. There's far more than you can really take in at a single sitting; there's so much that's fleeting or subliminal. But everything contributes, everything is as it must be to harmonize with the overall meaning.

This instinct for 'pure cinema' can perhaps be best appreciated in Lynch's use of that most basic element of the medium – the cut, the joining-together of two pieces of film. The first few scenes of *Blue Velvet* take place during the day. In the last such scene Jeffrey takes **the ear** to Detective Williams and then watches as the police search the field where he found it. Then there's a fade to black. The new scene begins with Jeffrey opening his bedroom door out of the darkness, the room behind him providing the only light as he walks down the stairs of the dark house. It's the perfect representation of the sort of journey on which he is about to embark – a person's quest for knowledge amid an all-consuming **darkness**. A fade to white at the end of the film after Jeffrey has killed Frank Booth signals that the journey through darkness is over and we can return to daylight.

The use of such fades is never neutral. They exploit the texture of the blackness. When Jeffrey hits Dorothy, they grapple with each other in slow motion, and an animal-like roar on the soundtrack, recalling the bugs in Mr Beaumont's lawn, brings out the primeval nature of their coupling. The roar continues after the screen has faded into blackness and then subsides. With the screen still black, Dorothy's faint, almost inaudible voice is heard saying, 'I have your disease in me now.' There's a similar effect a little later as Jeffrey sobs with shame as he recalls hitting Dorothy. The scene fades to black and the sound of his sobbing overlaps the darkness. In both cases the overlap pulls the metaphorical force of the darkness powerfully back into the preceding scene.

When Frank and his **gang** leave Ben's place to go on their joyride, the gang members vanish a split-second before the cut to their car burning up the road, so that momentarily all we see is the bare room where they once stood. The device perfectly captures the pell-mell pace of the evening, and Frank's diabolic, almost supernatural nature.

Although Lynch displays considerable ingenuity in these connections, he never pursues style for its own sake. It is always the meaning that determines the transition. One of the most effective connections is a simple cut from the church where Sandy has just told Jeffrey about her dream to a close-up of Jeffrey knocking on Dorothy's door. The juxtaposition conveys how casually Jeffrey can pass between the innocence of Sandy's world and the darkness of Dorothy's.

costume drama

Clothes function as a barometer of the characters' spiritual state. At the beginning of the film Jeffrey wears a pale shirt. When he tells Sandy of his plan to sneak into Dorothy's apartment he wears a black one, and on the night he carries the plan out he adds a dark tie with white flecks. At the end of the film, after Frank has been killed and order restored, he wears a white shirt with dark flecks.

The first time Sandy appears she is wearing a pale pink-and-white striped dress. When she goes out to **the Slow Club** with Jeffrey – the next stage in an unspoken courtship – she's wearing a rich-pink jersey. The beautiful rose-patterned dress she wears in the last stages of the film completes the picture of a girl flowering into womanhood.

Frank wears a black leather jacket when he visits Dorothy in her apartment – he's a creature of **darkness**. But the light shirt he wears over a dark vest at the Slow Club suggests a residual humanity. As he listens to Dorothy's song he is overwhelmed by emotion.

But Dorothy's dressing-up carries the greatest pathos. She likes herself so little that she does everything she can to hide herself away. Bathed in the lush red and blue light of the Slow Club, she wears her make-up like a mask.

Back in **Deep River Apartments** the luxuriant dark curls of her hair are revealed to be just a wig. She takes it off when she thinks she's alone, and it's a shock suddenly to see her own hair cropped so brutally short.

Whether it's the costume she wears for her nightclub act or the blue velvet gown she puts on as the object of Frank's vicious fantasies, Dorothy uses clothes as make-believe, a papering over of the cracks in her personality. What she wears or doesn't wear reflects her troubled, contradictory nature. She's either disguised in the mask and the robes of **the Blue Lady**, or she's naked, her madness exposed to the world. As long as she remains under Frank's spell there's no middle ground. Only at the very end, once Frank has been killed and her son restored to her, do we see her in ordinary everyday clothes.

See **Norris, Patricia**.

D

Dante (1265–1321)

'In the middle of the journey of our life I came to myself within a dark wood where the straight way was lost.' So begins Dante's *Inferno*. His way was barred by a lion, a wolf and a leopard – creatures symbolising the temptations of the world. Virgil guides Dante through the two lower realms of the next world, Hell and Purgatory. When they reach the Earthly Paradise Beatrice appears. Virgil leaves and Dante is led by Beatrice through the various celestial spheres to the supreme Heaven. Here he is granted for a brief moment an understanding of all mysteries and a vision of 'the Love that moves the sun and the other stars'.

Although he is denied the help of a guide, Jeffrey embarks on a similar journey. In **Deep River Apartments** he sees the creatures of Hell, and in Sandy he finds a counterpart to Beatrice's divine love, and together they are afforded a glimpse of 'the mysteries of love'.

darkness

It is the prevailing element, signifying ignorance and confusion. It also represents mystery. It announces the beginning of Jeffrey's quest to unravel a hidden world. The film, which begins in the daytime, switches to the night when Jeffrey, unable to contain his curiosity, takes an evening stroll over to Detective Williams's house to ask him about the severed **ear**. In an abstract sequence the camera plunges into the ear and burys itself in the darkness within.

Lynch uses darkness to map out the interior mood of his characters.

It's at its most intense after Jeffrey has hit Dorothy. It is the first time he has become aware of such evil in himself. As he gets ready to leave her apartment, there seem to be great lakes of blackness into which he could tumble and get lost for ever.

The forces of evil cling to darkness. 'Now it's dark . . .' is Frank's refrain. He says it in Dorothy's apartment before he abuses her; he says it too just before he sets off from Ben's place to beat up Jeffrey in **Meadow Lane**. (Lynch was so taken by the phrase that he used it again at the beginning of the Julee Cruise song 'Into the Night' on the *Twin Peaks* soundtrack.) With Frank's death the blue skies return, but, as this ending mirrors the film's beginning, there's an uneasy sense that so too could the darkness.

But darkness has a **dual** quality. It is the source of beauty. It provides the relief with which beauty can be recognised, and cloaks it in the mystery which is its essence. A church lit up in the night – it is the encompassing darkness that invests this image with loveliness. The first time Jeffrey meets Sandy she materialises out of the dark like a vision of a goddess. She belongs to it as much as Dorothy. For darkness is a place of dreams as much as nightmares, a place of inspiration. It's there in *Blue Velvet*'s most transcendent moment as Jeffrey and Sandy acknowledge their love for each other: 'Sometimes a wind blows and you and I float in love and kiss for ever in a darkness and the mysteries of love come clear.'

'In the cold light of day . . .' It's a lowering expression that offers no scope for poetry. It's the currency that the grown-ups deal in.

See **black-and-colour**.

Deep River Apartments

In **Dante**'s *Inferno* a river of blood separates lower Hell from upper Hell. The first level of Hell within this boundary is the 7th Circle, where the sins of violence are punished. In *Blue Velvet* the number 7 is associated with the places of darkness. Dorothy lives on the 7th floor of Deep River Apartments; and both **the Slow Club**, where Frank goes to hear her sing, and **Meadow Lane**, where he inflicts violence on his victims, are on Route 7.

In the 7th Circle of Hell reside those who inflict violence not only on others but also on themselves. According to the Dantean conception, both Frank and Dorothy belong there. The 7th Circle is guarded by the Minotaur, as Dorothy's apartment is watched over by the Yellow Man. Half man, half beast, the Minotaur represents the animal-like nature of violence. In their treatment of Dorothy both Frank and Jeffrey are likened to beasts.

See **710**.

Dern, Laura (b. 1966)

Her parents are the actors Bruce Dern and Cheryl Ladd, but her family is as notable for a more conservative pedigree: a cousin of her mother's was the playwright Tennessee Williams, and her paternal grandfather was secretary of war under Roosevelt and governor of Utah. Perhaps this august lineage accounts for the seriousness of approach that has characterised her own acting career and which was obvious from an early age.

Her first taste of the movies was banana-flavoured ice creams. When she was seven, she had to eat nine of them in nine takes for Martin Scorsese's *Alice Doesn't Live Here Any More*. To do that without throwing up was the sign of an actress, Scorsese told her mother, and, in spite of considerable success since, she has remained an actress rather than a star.

In *Teachers* she played a pregnant teenager who has an abortion. During the filming, she checked into an abortion clinic to get an idea of how the character would feel. In Peter Bogdanovich's *Mask* she was a blind girl who falls in love with a boy with a disfiguring and fatal bone disease. To prepare for the role she spent several days wearing a blindfold.

She enrolled at UCLA to study child psychology, but left to appear in the film *Smooth Talk*: 'I chose to act instead of having a college education, and I think that's why I like movies that educate me.' This attitude recalls Sandy's mixture of curiosity and level-headedness – the girl who wants to discover the adult world but without taking undue risks. If for Sandy Jeffrey offered an opportunity to learn things by proxy, for Dern it was acting, which 'makes you grow up. Through the roles you play, you learn about your true self.'

In *Smooth Talk* she played a bored teenager, who is seduced by a much older man. She is split between the pull of the adult world, and her fear of its dangers. The ambivalence required of the role anticipated *Blue Velvet*'s mood of uncertainty.

Because the character of Sandy is mostly looking on rather than taking an active part in the story herself, she could easily have seemed two-dimensional, but Dern's perceptive performance suggested her unexpressed, hidden side. Outwardly restrained, inwardly Sandy is agitated by some turbulent emotions. There's always something more than meets the eye about her. When she shows Jeffrey where Dorothy lives, it's partly her own curiosity but also a veiled flirtation. When her boyfriend Mike stumbles upon her rendezvous with Jeffrey and walks off upset, you can tell that she's bothered but also secretly quite pleased.

Dickerson, George

A veteran character actor of film and TV who has played numerous doctors, lawyers and policemen. He was a mortician in *Cutter's Way*, a sheriff in *Psycho II* and made several appearances as a police detective in *Hill Street Blues*. Playing a cop who has seen too much in *Blue Velvet* would have come easily to him. Other films include *No Mercy*, *Death*

Wish 4 – where he played a detective again – *After Dark, My Sweet* and *As Good as Dead*.

See **Williams, Detective**.

dogs

See **'Angriest Dog in the World, The'; comedy**.

Don

Dorothy's husband has his **ear** cut off, a bullet put through his head and blue velvet stuffed in his mouth, all because Frank loves his wife. We never see him alive, but he makes a memorable corpse – a *cadavre d'art* matched only by the coffee-table man in Lynch's film *Lost Highway*.

See **Van Gogh**.

Dorothy

She is a slave. Frank's assaults on her have become a domestic routine. Life at **710 Deep River Apartments** is a grotesque perversion of **family** values. Frank arrives at her apartment like an irritable paterfamilias home from work and expecting to find his dinner on the table. In what is clearly an often-repeated ritual, Dorothy fetches a small red chair, turns out the light and lights a candle in readiness for Frank to take possession of her.

This enslavement began as a desperate compliance with the kidnapper of her husband and son. They are the most precious things in her life; she has a photograph of them which she hides under a sofa. But Frank has pushed her so far off course that she has come to take pleasure in the pain he inflicts. At its root lies a sense of worthlessness and a longing for oblivion.

Not that Dorothy can have had an easy ride through life before

Frank came on the scene. One feels she's met too many of the wrong people and doesn't expect to be treated well. She doesn't know how to deal with people who treat her nicely. She wants Jeffrey to help her, but also to hurt her. She looks to him for comfort. She keeps calling him after her husband, Don, and thinks of him as a kind of guardian angel. 'I looked for you in my **closet** tonight,' she confides to him. 'It's crazy, I don't know where you come from but I like you.' But her self-esteem is too low for this to be enough. She begs him to hit her. It's not just her suicidal urge, but also a wish that he should expose his own vulnerability. For this is something she understands. This offers her the solace of shared experience.

Dorothy has a touching integrity – as she tells Jeffrey, she knows the difference between right and wrong – but like so many characters in David Lynch's films she has been victimised and conditioned by her surroundings. What's so frightening about the scenes in Deep River Apartments is witnessing the mechanism of abuse by which she passes on what she has suffered. 'How many times have you sneaked into girls' apartments and watched them undress?' she asks Jeffrey, and then she forces *him* to undress. 'Don't look at me!' she says uncertainly as she fondles him at knife-point, echoing the words that Frank has said to her.

By killing her husband, Frank finally pushes Dorothy over the brink. She turns up at Jeffrey's house, emerging naked from the bushes. Her misery is total. She has literally nothing to cover or protect her. She is as exposed and vulnerable as it is possible for a human being to be. Like the blue skies and white picket fences of **Lumberton**, so serene that they become sinister, Lynch turns a conventional image. Dorothy is the glamorous nightclub singer, the actress who plays her an international model, but her nudity is repellent and frightening.

When Isabella Rossellini played the part of Dorothy she imagined 'cows hanging in butchers' shops'. As she came out of the bushes, the picture she had in her mind 'was of that little girl hit by a napalm bomb in Vietnam. She had skin hanging off and she walked like that, completely naked down the street. The only thing you could see was pain.'

The scene was based on a real occurrence in Lynch's childhood:

When I was little, I think it was in Boise, Idaho, I was with my younger brother, and we saw a grown woman walking naked on the street. My brother started crying. And that was Dorothy, right there. It was so strange but it was also strange that my brother started crying. Because she was crazed, something bad had happened – we both knew she didn't even know where she was or that she was naked. The same as Dorothy.

Double Ed

Double Ed is – are? – two middle-aged black men who work in the Beaumont family hardware store. They are two people but are referred to as one. They are a tribute to inexplicable divination. One half of Double Ed is blind and walks with a white stick, but he knows where everything in the hardware store is kept. 'How many fingers?' asks Jeffrey as he holds up one hand. 'Four,' answers Double Ed. 'I still don't know how you do that!'

doubles

See **duality, double identity** and **doubles**.

Dourif, Brad

See **Raymond**.

drugs

See **Pabst Blue Ribbon**.

duality, double identity and doubles

> I always wanted to sneak into a girl's room at night and just
> watch her . . . the idea was that I would be watching her
> and I would see a clue, whether I knew it then or later, an
> important clue to a mystery, like a murder.

An element of creation is imagining an alternative life for oneself. In *Blue Velvet* Jeffrey is to an extent Lynch's alter ego. They both have their daydreams in diners. Lynch has spoken of Bob's Big Boy, Los Angeles, where ideas for movies would come to him; and Jeffrey tells Sandy of his plan to sneak into Dorothy's apartment in **Arlene**'s. 'It sounds like a good daydream,' says Sandy, 'but actually doing it is too weird, too dangerous.' Here is the difference. Lynch just has the daydream (as far as we know); Jeffrey actually does it.

When Lynch was growing up, he remembers longing for 'something out of the ordinary to happen. Something so that everyone will feel sorry for you. And you'll be like a victim. You know, if there was a tremendous accident and you were left alone.' This was another fantasy that he was able to live out vicariously – another imagining of an alternative life. There are both victims and orphans in *Blue Velvet* – Dorothy's son Donny, kidnapped and deprived of his mother; Jeffrey himself, whose father is struck down.

A strong dualistic pattern runs through *Blue Velvet*, with its concern for other lives, and double lives and split personalities. A son is a second self, and Jeffrey enters a strange new world after his father's seizure. When he visits Dorothy, she routinely calls him Don, a name that both her husband and son share. The identification encourages comparison. Little Don is Jeffrey's *dopplegänger* to the extent that both have been deprived of a parent, and Jeffrey will be kidnapped by Frank just as Don has been. This comparison with a child brings out the sense of Jeffrey's experience being a learning process on the way to adulthood.

Part of growing up is becoming like your father. When we see Jeffrey at home dressed like his father and watering his lawn it's a sign that he has begun to take on this second self.

By contrast Frank is the *doppelgänger* from hell. 'You're like me,' he taunts Jeffrey. And it's true. At **the Slow Club** he falls under the spell of Dorothy as Frank does; and he ends up hitting Dorothy as Frank does. Even in the very act of killing Frank Jeffrey's being like him, sending the kind of 'love letter' that once Frank had promised him ('You know what a love letter is? It's a bullet straight from my gun, fucker'). It's as if he's killing the evil side of himself.

In the world of *Blue Velvet* people lead double lives and possess dual natures. Jeffrey acts as a substitute for Dorothy's son but also offers the kind of help that she might expect of a husband. He is both a detective and a voyeur. He seeks both the sacred and the profane; he courts Sandy, yet at the same time he becomes infatuated with Dorothy. Jeffrey keeps the one **secret** from the other. And just as he shows two faces to the world, there are two sides warring within him. A destructive impulse vies with a positive one, just as his reckless curiosity vies with his fear and caution.

All the main characters must cope with such contradictory impulses. Sandy is as curious about the mystery of the severed **ear** as Jeffrey, yet as anxious not to be involved. Dorothy is a mother, yet as helpless as a child; she wants to be protected, yet tries to destroy herself; she hides away her marriage certificate as a treasured possession, yet takes a secret lover.

But it's in Frank that this war of opposites finds its most extreme form. In his ritual with Dorothy he can be both 'baby' and 'daddy', just as he looks upon **sex** and violence as the same. He stuffs the orifices of his victims with blue velvet, and cries 'Pretty, pretty!' as he kills them. The sadness is that, although his whole personality seems firmly set upon an axis of destruction, he does have intimations of a better life. There's a hint of this refined side as he sits in the Slow Club listening to Dorothy sing 'Blue Velvet'. But like a modern-day Jekyll, he downs his cocktail of **drugs** and drink, keeping himself for ever Mr Hyde.

Knowledge and experience are depicted as crucial ingredients in attaining a balance between the two warring sides of man's nature. In terms of Jeffrey's development as a character, the narrative of *Blue Velvet* seems to me like a seesaw pivoted on the night when Frank kidnaps him and beats him up. Jeffrey learns 'a lot in one night' and his behaviour changes accordingly. Before, he was eager to explore; afterwards, he prefers to stay at home. Before, he delighted in revealing to Sandy what he had discovered; afterwards, he prefers to keep things hidden, revelation becoming a sober, reluctant matter as finally he feels obliged to tell Detective Williams what he's seen.

A dualistic scheme operates at every level in *Blue Velvet*. There's Sandy's dream – with our world, which is dark, and the other world, from which the **robins** of love come. It's in the opposition between the safety of the suburbs and the danger of Lincoln Street, between the good cop Detective Williams and the bad cop Detective Gordon, the Yellow Man; even in the decor of Dorothy's apartment, with the old-fashioned two-pronged aerial that sits on top of the television and the two sickly pot plants that sit on a ledge on either side of a wall light.

It's there in the end that mirrors the beginning – the yellow and red flowers against the white picket fence, the red fire engine gliding by with its waving fireman, and the camera finally returning to the blue sky from where it first descended. Indeed, the whole second half of the film is like a reverse mirror image of the first. So Jeffrey is glad to stay at home when before he was anxious to get away from it. So Dorothy comes out naked from the bushes of Jeffrey's house, just as in the first half Jeffrey had sneaked into **the closet** of her apartment; as Dorothy had forced Jeffrey to undress, now Jeffrey sees to it that she is covered up. The dark world visits the light, as previously the light had visited the dark. So, with Jeffrey in danger, Sandy finally hurries to **Deep River Apartments**, when before she had shied away from the place. And so the camera pulls out of Jeffrey's ear into the sunlight, as previously it had plunged into the **darkness** of the severed ear, and the robin with the bug in its beak counterpoints the bugs beneath Mr Beaumont's lawn.

In the reunions of the final sequence there's an almost comic ode to symmetry, twindom and balance. The Williamses have visited the Beaumonts for lunch. Just as Jeffrey and Sandy are together, so we see, looking interchangeable, the two fathers together in the garden and the two mothers together in the house. And finally we see Dorothy reunited with her son.

See **colours**.

duck, the

A wooden duck sits in front of a photograph of Sandy in her father's study. We see it before we meet Sandy herself, when Jeffrey visits Detective Williams in the evening after discovering the severed **ear**. This duck is a cryptic tribute to the harmony that Sandy represents. In interviews about his work, Lynch has often used the duck as a symbol of artistic pefection: 'How a duck is made and where the different things are on a duck can give you a clue to a more or less perfect composition for a painting. If you could interpret a duck, if you could work with the rules of a duck, you could get something close to a well-composed **painting**.'

Dune

Watching *Dune* is an ordeal. It's like attending a dinner party where you don't understand the language the other guests are speaking. You try to pick up what you can, but feel helpless as the conversation leaves you far behind. There was too much to explain in too short a time. The producers' need to have a marketable commodity dictated

a length of a little over two hours. If Lynch had had his way it would
have been nearer four, and probably it needed eight.

It was a noble failure which foundered on its determination to be
true to the original book regardless of the severe handicap of the
running time. The cuts required to squeeze the narrative into two
hours resulted in a disjointed, telescoped movie that felt like a digest
of a much longer film. But also, in being faithful to the Frank Herbert
novel, Lynch accepted many absurdities that he might otherwise have
questioned. The first half of the film is gruelling but fascinating as
Lynch builds a 'strange world' and introduces its characters, but the
second half lapses into action movie clichés as Paul Atreides leads his
band of freedom fighters against the evil Harkonnens. A David Lean,
not Lynch, was needed to bring conviction to such material.

But in so many ways *Dune* anticipates *Blue Velvet*. Both films depict
a 'strange world', even if the strange world of *Blue Velvet* lies behind
a veil of normality. Lynch lingers over the bugs crawling beneath
the grass, or the ant-encrusted **ear** discovered in the undergrowth,
or the fatal wounds of Frank's victims with the same obsessive thrill
that he explores the textures of the Galaxy, whether the evil Baron
Harkonnen's suppurating pustules, the ribbed rubber stillsuits of the
Fremens or the fleshy, brain-like substance of the Spacing Guild
Navigator – horrifyingly plausible as an organic growth, a sort of
cross between the Elephant Man and the baby in **Eraserhead**.

Kyle MacLachlan, as Paul Atreides, is the young man who must
emerge from out of the shadow of his father, Duke Leto. Before they
embark for the planet Arrakis, his father tells him: 'A person needs new
experiences. They draw on something deep inside, allowing them
to grow. Without change something sleeps inside us, and seldom
awakens. The sleeper must awaken.' This phrase, 'The sleeper must
awaken', becomes as much a refrain in *Dune* as 'It's a strange world'
is in *Blue Velvet*.

Eventually Paul Atreides does awaken and, stepping into the shoes of his murdered father, leads the fight against the Harkonnens. The town of **Lumberton**, North Carolina, is hardly as exotic as the planet Arrakis, but Jeffrey undergoes a similar process of initiation. After Mr Beaumont has been struck down he steps into *his* father's shoes and eventually contends with Frank, as Paul Atreides does the evil Baron Harkonnen.

The grotesque baron seems like a prototype for Frank and the larger-than-life villains that would follow in Lynch's subsequent films – Bobby Peru in *Wild at Heart*, Bob in *Twin Peaks* and Mr Ed in *Lost Highway*. In each case the evil is exemplified in a sadistic and omniverous **sexual** appetite. Mr Ed is the porno king, Bobby Peru, 'a big old jackrabbit', boasts of his prowess, and 'I'll fuck anything that moves!' screams Frank Booth. His abuse of Dorothy recalls the Baron's humiliation of Paul Atreides' mother. 'I want to spit once on your head,' he drools lasciviously, 'just some spittle in your face.' And Lynch characteristically delights in showing the globule of saliva splatting on to its target. But gobbing on the wives of his enemies is just one of the ways in which the Baron takes his pleasure. He also lusts after his own nephew and drinks the blood of a pubescent boy. His cultivation of blue tulips is as much a symbol of his unnatural, fetishistic appetite as the blue velvet is of Frank's. Such was its cornucopia of evil that Lynch was able to call upon several of *Dune*'s supporting villains for his next film. The Harkonnens Brad Dourif and Jack Nance became Frank's sidekicks Raymond and Paul, and Dean Stockwell's treacherous Dr Wellington Yueh became Ben.

Lynch was as fascinated by the inner world of his characters as by the exotic galaxy in which they lived. The people of the planet Caitan can communicate by telepathy, and the hero Paul Atreides possesses a messiah's intuition. When Paul first arrives on the arid planet of Arrakis – otherwise known as Dune – Dr Kynes, his father's adviser and expert on the ways of Arrakis, is astonished to find that the boy wears his desert suit like a native. He asks Paul who told him to wear it in such a manner. 'No one. It seemed the right way.' In *Blue Velvet* Sandy's first meeting with Jeffrey provides an echo of this encounter. 'Are you the one that found the ear?' Sandy asks. 'Yeah. How do you know,' replies Jeffrey. 'I just know.'

Paul Atreides may have to fight the evil Harkonnens, but he is depicted as also having to struggle against the fear within himself. In *Blue Velvet* Jeffrey must contend with the evil Frank Booth but also come to terms with his dark side. In both films Lynch explored the mind's vulnerability and its power. 'I walk with you in dreams,' Frank threatens Jeffrey, while it is in dreams that Paul Atreides can envision the future.

Getting inside people's heads, this is Lynch's long-term project. In *Dune* he did it crudely. Voice-over is used throughout to convey what the characters are thinking. So when Paul Atreides meets Dr Kynes for the first time, we hear his thoughts as he sizes up his father's adviser: 'He must be a Fremen. Or in with them. He's studying us.' It was about as subtle as the thought bubbles in cartoons, but it revealed an instinct for capturing psychic experience which Lynch would harness to better effect in *Blue Velvet*.

Dunham, Duwayne

He began in films as an apprentice editor on *One Flew Over the Cuckoo's Nest*. He then worked as an assistant to George Lucas for eight years. He was an assistant editor on *The Empire Strikes Back* and then an editor on *The Return of the Jedi*. After editing *Blue Velvet* he went on to edit the pilot of the *Twin Peaks* TV series, for which he won an Emmy, and *Wild at Heart*. The collaboration with Lynch ended because Dunham wanted to be a director himself, and Lynch gave him the opportunity to direct three episodes of *Twin Peaks*.

Then in 1991 Dunham directed *Homeward Bound: The Incredible Journey* for Walt Disney Pictures. It was a live-action adventure story

about two dogs and a cat who trek across the American wilderness to
rejoin their family in San Francisco. The animals talked, with Michael
J. Fox, Don Ameche and Sally Field providing the voices, and the
film was dubbed by the critics 'Look Who's Barking'. Such a typically
saccharine Disney tale might have seemed a rather startling change of
direction had not dogs featured so memorably in both *Blue Velvet* and
Wild at Heart. When the human beings in Lynch's films had behaved
so abominably, there was even a certain logic in finally giving up on
them and making a film in which animals were given pride of place.
Dunham made one more feature film, *Little Giants*, in 1994, and has
since directed episodes of the American TV series *JAG*, *Seventh Heaven*
and *Beyond Belief*.

See **connections**.

E

ear, the

Jeffrey's discovery of a severed ear in a field is the beginning of the mystery. It belongs to Dorothy's husband, Don, whom Frank Booth has kidnapped along with Dorothy's son. It is a warning to Dorothy that she should comply with Frank's wishes.

'It had to be an ear because it's an opening,' commented Lynch. 'An ear is wide and, as it narrows, you can go down into it. And it goes somewhere vast.' But it is also appropriate because perception is such a strong theme in the film. It's apt too that it should be Frank who cuts the ear off. He fears knowledge and seeks to efface it.

Gossip has it that Lynch kept an ear in his pocket when he was filming *Twin Peaks*. True or not, this story seems entirely plausible. An ear is as perfect a talisman as a rabbit's paw. Or a piece of blue velvet – soft and leathery, the feel must be similar.

In *Reservoir Dogs* Quentin Tarantino pays homage to *Blue Velvet* with a scene in which a psychopathic gangster, Mr Blonde, cuts off the ear of a captured policeman. Like Frank beating up Jeffrey in **Meadow Lane**, Mr Blonde does it to music.

eighties, the

There are enough details to make it clear that the setting is contemporary to the mid-eighties – the Beaumonts' television, even Jeffrey's boxer shorts – but it can feel a little as if **Lumberton** has wilfully chosen to turn its back on the decade, stubbornly preferring to cling on to its old cars and telephones.

Blue Velvet challenges your memory of the past. Surely, hadn't computers started to creep into the workplace by the mid-eighties? But they are absent from the town's police station. It's a place where even an IBM golfball would seem unnecessarily advanced, the officers preferring to clunk away on something heavy and metallic. And in the Beaumonts' hardware store Double Ed rings up purchases on an old mechanical cash-till. Outside the store there's a sign which says 'ANTIQUES'. They are everywhere in Lumberton. This is a community of people keen to affirm that the old ways are the best ways.

See **period**.

electricity

It's a mysterious, invisible but immensely powerful force. When Jeffrey visits **Deep River Apartments** a shorting neon sign in the foyer suggests the malign spirit that has taken hold of the building. After Frank has been killed, two bulbs in Dorothy's apartment blow. It's like the breaking of the enchanted castle's spell. It recalls the breaking of another spell at the end of *Wild at Heart*. When Sailor takes the Good Witch's advice and returns to Lula, a photograph of the wicked witch of a mother who has been trying to keep them apart goes up in smoke.

Elephant Man, The

It was in *The Elephant Man*, with its conventional narrative, that the **duality** so notable in *Blue Velvet* and Lynch's subsequent films first began to emerge. Also like *Blue Velvet*, the film was about **voyeurism**.

In Victorian London the surgeon Frederick Treves rescues the hideously deformed John Merrick from a freak show. At first silent and uncommunicative, Merrick is discovered to be a man of considerable charm and intelligence. He is given permanent sanctuary in the hospital where Treves works, and in the very short life that is left him enjoys the respect and affection of London society.

The narrative pattern of *The Elephant Man* anticipated *Blue Velvet*, except that it progressed from **darkness** to light instead of the other way around – finding beauty behind ugliness, instead of corruption behind an apparent serenity. *The Elephant Man* was an assignment rather than a personal project, but the simplicity of the story gave Lynch a chance to develop his vision. A moral awareness not obvious in his previous film, **Eraserhead**, emerges. As he depicts a dirty grim city where a vicious underclass cowers in the shadow of hulking, steam-belching machinery, there's a powerful sense of humanity being shaped for good or ill by its environment.

In *Blue Velvet* Frank lives in the industrial part of town. When one night Jeffrey follows him to his apartment we hear the sound of infernal machinery pounding away and, amid smoke and flames, see its shadow on the wall. In this brief abstract moment *The Elephant Man*'s world of dark satanic mills slips into *Blue Velvet*.

The way we are treated is crucial to what we become. In this respect John Merrick anticipates Dorothy. As an exhibit at the freak show, Merrick turns in on himself and, in accordance with the savage treatment that Bytes, his fairground owner, metes out, becomes little more than a dumb animal, easily mistaken for the imbecile the surgeon Treves at first believes him to be. In the hospital, nurtured and surrounded by kindness, he blossoms.

Dorothy must put up with her own Bytes in the shape of Frank Booth. She seems as much a prisoner in **Deep River Apartments** as Merrick was in the fair. Subjected to Frank's brutality, her personality comes apart, she turns in on herself like the Elephant Man. By killing

Frank, Jeffrey rescues Dorothy from his evil influence much as Treves rescued Merrick from Bytes. She too has a chance to blossom again.

In the surgeon Treves can be found the traces of a moral ambiguity of character that Lynch would push to its limits in *Blue Velvet*. As Jeffrey becomes more and more obsessed by the case, Sandy declares of him, 'I don't know if you're a detective or a pervert.' The words recall those of Treves when he agonises over his motives in bringing John Merrick to the hospital. As his patient becomes the talk of first the medical world and then polite society, Treves is troubled by the thought that he may be little better than the showman Bytes – the only difference being that he parades his charge before a better class of customer. 'Am I a good man or a bad man?' he asks himself.

This **dualistic** scheme finds form on a larger scale in the hospital itself. It's intended to be a sanctuary, but after hours an unscrupulous porter smuggles gawping, mocking visitors into the helpless Merrick's room. His life is starkly divided between light and **darkness**, between the civility of the privileged who pay their respects during the day and the abuse of the mob who invade his privacy at night. Similarly, in *Blue Velvet*'s **Lumberton** the nightmare world of Deep River Apartments is just a short walk from Jeffrey's pleasant neighbourhood.

Merrick's nobility of spirit is sustained through his various sufferings by the example and memory of his mother, and he becomes the '**child**' of the hospital, which provides him with love, respect and care. There's as strong a feel here for the **family**'s importance and its vulnerability as there is in *Blue Velvet*. Merrick is kidnapped from his 'family' by Bytes, as Dorothy's son Donny is kidnapped by Frank. Merrick carries around with him a portrait of his mother. 'She has the face of an angel,' he tells Mr and Mrs Treves. In the same way, Dorothy treats the photograph of her husband and son as a precious object. It helps to sustain her through the nightmare of her enslavement to Frank Booth.

Both *Blue Velvet* and *The Elephant Man* work as **fairy tales**. In the moving finale of the latter, John Merrick attends a pantomime in which, at the wave of a good fairy's wand, beasts are turned into princes.

Elmes, Frederick

When he was small his father let him borrow his Leica camera. He fell in love with taking pictures and went on to study photography at the Rochester Institute of Technology. His idea was to become a photo-journalist, but after discovering the films of Fellini, Antonioni and Bergman he decided to become a film-maker instead. He studied film at New York University, then in 1971 joined the American Film Institute (AFI) Center in Los Angeles. Here he met David Lynch, and took over as cinematographer on *Eraserhead*, when nine months into its five-year production the original cinematographer, Herb Cardwell, had to pull out. While he was at the AFI Elmes met John Cassavetes, and he went on to photograph for him *Killing of a Chinese Bookie* and *Opening Night*.

His work stands out in contrast to the just too perfect, pin-sharp lighting of mainstream Hollywood. *Blue Velvet* impresses for the visual transitions of atmosphere from the eerie brightness of sunny **Lumberton** to the sepulchral gloom of Dorothy's apartment. Elmes has spoken of lighting as having the same logical function as **music** in determing **mood**: 'Both evoke very direct emotional responses from viewers. Lighting is connected with the emotions. There is no separating them. When I view a scene, whether it's in a movie or real life, I'm affected emotionally by the feeling of the light.' This sensibility to mood and an appreciation of mystery – an understanding of photography as **painting** with **darkness** as much as with light – made him a perfect Lynch **collaborator**: 'By not explaining everything with light, darkness gives my imagination an opening. So sometimes I choose to hold back light in areas of the

frame, because I don't want to explain the image that clearly. I want
to make the audience imagine, and fish for what's out there.'

Elmes received the National Society of Film Critics Award for Best
Cinematography for *Blue Velvet* and went on to photograph Lynch's
Wild at Heart. Subsequent work has included Jim Jarmusch's *Night on
Earth* and Ang Lee's *The Ice Storm*.

Eraserhead

Eraserhead can be regarded as a companion piece to *Blue Velvet*. Both,
more obviously than any of Lynch's other features, draw on his own
life. Henry, the 'hero' of *Eraserhead*, was as much Lynch's **alter ego**
as later Jeffrey would be in *Blue Velvet*. *Eraserhead* was Lynch's
'Philadelphia' film, feeding on his experience of being a young
father living with his wife and child in a poor part of that city. The
Deep River Apartments and Lincoln Street of *Blue Velvet*, as well as
the industrial district where Frank lives and **Meadow Lane**, belong
to this *Eraserhead* world, but Lynch added a contrasting dimension
by returning to the idyll of his childhood. We see too the blue skies,
white picket fences and pretty houses of small-town America.

This **dualistic** outlook – such a notable feature of all his films since
Blue Velvet – is absent from *Eraserhead*. It's a monotone world. Henry's
a languid, listless young man on a seemingly endless 'vacation' – a
vacation of the most literal kind, for the life he leads is empty. He
spends his days mooning about his flat. Not even the news that he
has become a father impinges on his apathy. His wife lives with him
briefly until she gets sick of the baby's crying and goes back to stay
with her parents.

Henry is left alone to attend to the offspring, a premature, mewling
creature swaddled in a bandage. There's no plot because Henry's going
nowhere. We just share his stagnation for a while. He's the kind of
person who can spend a day staring at the ceiling. His only amusement

is to play over and over again a scratched record of pier organ music. His most meaningful experiences occur in his daydreams and fantasies. He finds a kind of guardian angel in his radiator – as Dorothy finds Jeffrey in her cupboard. 'In heaven everything's fine. You have your things, and I have mine,' sings the Lady in the Radiator, slightly off-key, over and over again.

Henry's whole world is out of tune. His clothes don't quite fit, doors slam just a little too loudly, electricity sockets sizzle with sparks, lamps cast feeble pools of light. Henry's stunted existence is in keeping with his environment. He inhabits a grey industrial landscape in which the sun never shines. *Eraserhead* conveys a **mood** from which no one who must live in a city is protected – the days when blight seems to be everywhere. This is the atmosphere of the world that Dorothy inhabits too. I don't know if Sartre ever visited Philadelphia, but when he went on to describe in *La Nausée* 'those strange districts where cities are manufactured' he could easily have been writing of Henry's neighbourhood, or Lincoln Street or Meadow Lane. These districts are 'near goods stations, tram depots, slaughter-houses, and gasometers. Two days after a downpour, when the whole city is moist in the sunshine and radiates damp heat, they are still cold, they keep their mud and puddles.'

There is something rather loving about the way in which Lynch depicts Henry's static existence. He captures the allure of limbo. In Henry's habitat, a place where you could crawl under a rock and go to sleep for ever, there are the deathly joys of Lethe. Lynch, fascinated by its texture, is drawn to Henry's world in spite of its dangers, and *Eraserhead* is as much an expression of his curiosity as of any fears. In visiting Henry's world for a while, he's like Jeffrey, helplessly fascinated, exploring the dismal Deep River Apartments.

Dorothy, listless in her broken-down building, could easily live round the corner from Henry. Both are mired in the same morass of gloom and apathy. Henry has found a modus vivendi, while

Dorothy is in despair. But her misery has an identifiable cause – the kidnapping of her **child** – and events will bring about its end. Henry's apathy is more deep-seated; his separation from his wife and his disturbed experience of fatherhood seem less a cause of his state of mind than a symptom. The nightmare of *Eraserhead* is that of a functioning dysfunctional world. While the elevator in Deep River Apartments is broken down, Henry's still rumbles up, albeit painfully slowly, to the grim apartment from which you just can't imagine him ever escaping.

The coda of *Blue Velvet*, in which Dorothy sits in a pleasant park reunited with her child and enjoying at least a brief respite of happiness, is impossible to imagine for Henry, whose life seems barred from progression. Anaesthetised and stunted, he is spared Dorothy's misery but also denied her chance of redemption.

Because it suggests that, in spite of all the trouble in the world, we can achieve a degree of wisdom, I find *Blue Velvet* – finally – an uplifting and hopeful film. It's moved on from the moral dead end of *Eraserhead* – it's as if Lynch himself has found some answers since. It has a narrative, it's going somewhere. Lynch's films move at different speeds, reflecting different levels of anxiety. *Eraserhead* is stationary: Henry hardly strays out of his neighbourhood. *Blue Velvet* is an uneasy walk across town from the cosy suburb where Jeffrey lives to troubled districts like Lincoln and Meadow Lane. And *Wild at Heart* is a pell-mell dash across a whole country.

F

fairy tales

Blue Velvet is a modern-day fairy tale. All the ingredients are there: the woods that surround **Lumberton**; **Deep River Apartments**, a kind of enchanted castle from which the prince must rescue the Sleeping Beauty; and wolves. The storyline is not so different from that of 'Little Red Riding Hood'. When Little Red Riding Hood has been rescued from the wolf she promises: 'I'll never again leave the path and run into the forest by myself when mother has said I mustn't.' Just as her curiosity leads her into the clutches of the wolf, Jeffrey's leads to his perilous encounter with Frank. Both tales warn of the dangers that await those who disregard the advice of their elders.

The finale of *Blue Velvet* reminds me a little of a Christmas pantomime. Frank hunting down Jeffrey in his well-dressed man disguise resembles the wolf wearing granny's clothes. 'Here I come, ready or not!' he cries as he fits a silencer to his gun. With Jeffrey hiding in Dorothy's **closet**, the situation is pretty much the same as that of the 'Three Little Pigs'. 'I'll huff and I'll puff and I'll blow your house down!' says the wolf, while Frank, his modern-day counterpart, huffs and puffs into his **gas** mask in order to get high before pouncing. But in fairy-tale fashion Jeffrey proves himself by outwitting Frank. He has managed to lure Frank away from his hiding place for long enough to get hold of a gun from the pocket of the Yellow Man. When Frank opens the closet door he is slain by a

young hero like all the countless wolves and ogres and witches
before him.

families

Everything that happens in *Blue Velvet* does so within a family
framework. It's the prevailing order. The film begins with Jeffrey
coming home to run the Beaumont store after his father's seizure. Detective Williams, the officer who investigates the mystery
of the severed **ear**, is also Sandy's father and is seen mostly at
his home.

The Williams family and the Beaumont family remind me of
those first words in *Anna Karenina*: 'All happy families are alike
. . .' They are lightly sketched, to the extent that – as Pauline
Kael pointed out – when the mothers are seen together, they seem
almost like identical twins, '. . . but each unhappy family is unhappy
in its own way.' When Jeffrey visits **Deep River Apartments** he
stumbles upon both a broken family and a perverted one. Frank
has kidnapped Dorothy's husband and son and supplanted them,
imposing on Dorothy his own vicious domestic routine. As monstrous
as his behaviour may be, it says something for the ancient pull
of the family that he should go to such lengths to have one of
his own.

But Frank's notions of family are deeply confused. He's torn
between contradictory desires. He wants to be both father and son.
While the one role offers him the assurance that he is in control, the
other expresses a a primeval yearning for love and nurture. In the
act of **sex** he cannot distinguish between the two: 'Baby wants blue
velvet,' he pleads, and he calls Dorothy mommy, yet as he climaxes
cries, 'Daddy's home!'

In Deep River Apartments Jeffrey finds himself pulled into this
family from hell. As the writer J. G. Ballard has commented, 'This is

the story of **children** who sneak into their parents' bedroom while they're out and hide in the cupboard. And when the parents come back the children see rather more than they bargained for.'

This sense of Jeffrey as the surrogate son is at its strongest when Frank kidnaps him and takes him on a 'joy ride'. It's like a family outing. Frank and Dorothy sit in the front of the car like mummy and daddy, Jeffrey their son in the back, with Frank's **gang** the other siblings. 'He's a pussy!' says one of the gang of Jeffrey as they drive to Ben's. 'Yeah, but he's our pussy. Right, tits?' says Frank, addressing Dorothy.

The drama unfolds according to an Oedipal logic, whereby Jeffrey usurps daddy's place, makes love to mommy and kills daddy in the end. Jeffrey takes not only Frank's place, but that of Dorothy's husband and son too. Dorothy even several times calls him 'Don', a name her husband and son share.

Ben's place offers another permutation of the perverse family. It's where Dorothy's kidnapped son is kept, looked after by Ben's fat ladies. It's a meeting ground for orphans and prodigals and strays, who under Ben's sway come to form a quasi-family of their own. Behind a closed door Dorothy is allowed to see her son. She comes out in despair because he questions her love for him. In her anguish can be found the damage that these corrupt families wreak.

Blue Velvet is not a didactic film, but if you wanted to look for a moral, one that you could easily draw is the importance of a healthy family life. Achieving such a thing requires a balance in the ever-shifting tensions that exist within families. Lynch's own memory of growing up is of a happy family life which, however, in its very ordinariness made him long for something awful to happen. The recollection brings to mind Jeffrey, who to appreciate his family had first to break away from it and taste an alternative life.

fifties, the

The decade in which Lynch grew up and **America** was most inclined to think it was a wonderful life, even if it wasn't. *Blue Velvet* is full of fifties archetypes – cars, diners, the girl next door – that reflect Lynch's nostalgia for the time.

See *It's a Wonderful Life*; **Lynch, David**; **period**.

Frank

Can you imagine anything more dangerous than a two-year-old with a gun? Well, that's Frank. Parents of young children will recognise many aspects of his behaviour – the temper tantrums, the nameless fears, the need to control. Like most of the two-year-olds I know, he's teetering on a tightrope edge of irreconcilable desires, and falling off all the time.

He has failed completely to learn those lessons that most of us began to master as toddlers. He's the prisoner of his emotions. He loves, he hates, and cannot distinguish between the two. He's a stunted creature, oblivious of the difference between right and wrong, even fearing the knowledge that might give him an inkling, as a beast fears fire.

In everything he embraces ignorance and **darkness**. 'Don't look at me!' he screams over and over again at Dorothy during their vicious coupling. He calls her 'Mommy' – having kidnapped her **child** he wants to supplant him – and talks of 'coming home', as if his most urgent desire is to return to the un-reason of the womb.

Blue velvet. He carries a piece around with him like a child's comforter, and we see him on the verge of tears as he listens to Dorothy sing the song. It's as if this man of instant animal desires is longing for some earlier, more innocent time. No one loves the golden oldies more than Frank. The songs he listens to are from a lost past and also about a lost past. 'When she left gone was the glow of blue

velvet,' sings Bobby Vinton, 'but in my heart there will always be . . .'
And it's the same sentiment on the tape that Frank carries around with
him like a talisman. 'In dreams I talk with you,' sings Roy Orbison.
'But just before the dawn I awake and find you're gone.'

What was Frank like when he was young? Surely something awful
must have happened. Perhaps he was kidnapped by a vicious gangster
who raped his mother and cut off his father's **ear**. It would have to be
something like that to explain him – is he now visiting on Dorothy's
son what he himself has suffered?

Although he certainly is a villain, this sense of his suffering makes
me hesitate to call him one. I have to confess that, having watched
Blue Velvet many times now, I've even grown rather fond of him.
He has a generous and big-hearted side. When he visits Ben's place
he tells his **gang** to get Ben a beer too, and he invites Ben's friends
to join him on his joy ride. His guilelessness is appealing. Instead
of 'Lets Play!' it's 'Lets go fuck!' He may demand that everything
should be on his terms, but he does want his friends to have fun
too. I wouldn't want to meet him and it's hard not to feel that
the only good Frank is a dead Frank – you can't imagine him ever
struggling free of his murderous existence – but how refreshing after
the stultifying and inert primness of small-town America to find an
honest man who says what he thinks. As Dennis Hopper put it, 'Frank
. . . well, he may be kind of sick – think of the **drugs** in his system,
that's his gig – but he's for real.'

Although I certainly did at first, I no longer think of Frank as evil.
In the grip of evil maybe, but therefore to be pitied. I'm even moved,
if frightened too, by the degree of his love. We should take him at his
word when he speaks of his bullets as love letters. There's something of
the Edward Scissorshands about him in the way he can communicate
deep feeling only through violence. Depraved as he may be, Frank
retains a humanity that can elicit our sympathy. He brings back the
pathetic child murderer in Fritz Lang's *M* – his heart-rending cry 'I

can't help it!' Whatever suffering he may inflict on other people, it's *his* tragedy too.

frank language

When BBC television broadcast *Blue Velvet* for the first time, a woman's voice, sounding formidably well educated and serious, warned that the film was 'a highly original and sometimes shocking exploration of the relationship between good and evil'. She went on: 'It contains disturbing scenes of violence and extremely frank language, which some viewers may be offended by.' I wonder if she realised just how accurate she was being. 'Fuck' is uttered many times in *Blue Velvet*, but nearly always by Frank Booth. Were it not for Frank, *Blue Velvet* might have seemed as remarkable for its absence of foul language at a time when Hollywood had become used to using expletives indiscriminately.

G

gangs

Gangs come in threes in *Blue Velvet*. Just as Frank has his henchmen Raymond, Hunter and Paul, Mike has his three mates, Ben his three fat ladies, and Sandy her three girlfriends from school.

In the script Frank just had two henchmen, Raymond and Paul. The third, Hunter, although he does not say a word, was added when the film was shot. Probably there was nothing significant in the presence of threes – it just seemed right, like Dorothy's three companions in *The Wizard of Oz*. It's the smallest crowd you can have, and Lynch, with his passion for texture and detail, would have appreciated the opportunity it afforded to depict group behaviour but still to individuate with intimacy.

gas

Whenever Frank Booth wants to heighten an act of **sex** or violence – and they amount to much the same thing in his crazed mind – he takes out a plastic mask and inhales **gas**. David Lynch had specified this gas as helium, which, according to the script, 'makes Frank's voice very high and strange sounding'. In this high voice Frank calls Dorothy 'Mommy' and pleads, 'Baby wants to fuck.' But then in his normal voice he commands: 'GET READY TO FUCK!' The script direction reads: 'Loud, but normal – like an army order to himself.'

Frank alternates between the two voices, and Lynch's intention seems to have been to suggest an individual split between two personalities – the domineering man and the needy **child**.

Dennis Hopper, with his personal knowledge of the effect of **drugs**, found Lynch's choice of gas implausible and suggested that he treat it as nitrous oxide instead, a gas which would heighten Frank's aggression. The result was a chilling whine halfway between Frank's normal voice and a baby's, which was disturbing but blurred the concept of two personalities. In a television interview Hopper expressed curiosity as to how he might have sounded had he played the gas scenes as Lynch originally intended. You can get some idea by running a print of the film fast through a viewing machine, as I found myself doing on one occasion. Frank sounds like Mickey Mouse; the effect is comic, but strangely compelling.

When Dorothy is rushed off to hospital in an ambulance she's trussed in a stretcher, and a gas mask just like Frank's is fixed to her face. The notion of the same object used to such contrary purposes is characteristic of Lynch.

genre

As Lynch put it himself: 'I love 47 genres in one film. I hate one-thing films. And I love B movies. But why not have three or four Bs running together? Like a little hive!' So *Blue Velvet* is a coming-of-age film, a thriller and a detective story, but also it's a **fairy tale** and a **love story**, a tragedy yet a comedy too. Lynch has often spoken of the inadequacy of words accurately to convey an experience, yet none the less seems more than happy to speak of his films in terms of sweeping genre labels – he once described *Lost Highway* as a '21st century *noir* horror film'. In this apparent contradiction can be traced a fascination with the contrast between life's apparent simplicity and actual complexity – the beautiful green lawn that is actually a forest of beetles.

Gordon, Detective

See **Yellow Man, the**.

H

happy ending?

It's a happy ending of the most provisional kind. Sandy and Jeffrey see not the thousands of **robins** that represent love in Sandy's dream, but just one with a bug in its beak. The sequence that follows builds on this unsettling note. The film ends as it begins, with yellow tulips against a white-picket fence, a red fire engine, and then red roses. So although we may finally see, in the very last scene of all, Dorothy reunited with her son, the circularity suggests that the **darkness** could return all over again. Dorothy's expression is joyful as her son runs into her arms, but then, briefly, it's as if a ghost walked across her soul, reminding her of a tormented past that she can never completely escape. Accompanying that momentary look of disquiet, we hear the last words of *Blue Velvet* – both the song and the film: 'And I can still see blue velvet through my tears.'

Henri, Robert (1865–1929)

A turn-of-the-century American painter who had studied at the Pennsylvania Academy of Fine Arts in Philadelphia – as Lynch would do nearly a century later – and then taught at the New York School of Art. Henri believed that art had value only to the extent that it offered an insight into life, and that therefore all aspects of life were worthy of depiction. He sent his students out into the streets of New York's Lower East Side to record the struggles of the immigrant community.

'Art for life's sake' was his motto. He believed that it should not be an academic or rarefied calling, but one intimately concerned with life and death issues.

While Lynch was still a high-school student in Virginia, his artist friend Bushnell Keeler recommended Henri's book *The Art Spirit* to him: It 'became . . . my Bible, because that book made the rules for the art life'. With its stress on the subjective impression over the representational, it offers an insight into Lynch's attitude. 'The great artist,' Henri wrote, 'has not reproduced nature, but has expressed by his extract the most choice sensation it has produced upon him.' Lynch's preference for **mood** over narrative is in tune with Henri's philosophy. 'Low art is just telling things, as, there is the night,' wrote Henri. 'High art gives the feel of night. The latter is nearer reality although the former is a copy.'

Henri might almost have been taking *Blue Velvet* as an example, so crammed is it with the 'feel of night'. **Darkness** is its special element. One thinks of Jeffrey and Sandy strolling through the streets after dark, the street lamps casting mysterious patterns of light on the canopy of leaves above; or the illuminated buildings of the neighbourhood that stand out like havens against the vastness of the pitch-black sky. These are everyday things, but Lynch sees them anew, investing them with an epic quality.

It's pleasing to discover that Henri's name was an alias, so wedded is Lynch to the notion that 'things are not what they seem'. He was born Robert Henry Cozad. His family lived in Nebraska, but fled to Colorado after his father shot an employee in a gambling duel. His parents assumed the names Mr and Mrs Lee and passed off their two sons as adopted.

Hopper, Dennis (b. 1936)

When Lynch began to shoot *Blue Velvet* the part of Frank Booth had still not been cast. Hopper had been considered, but dismissed because of his reputation for alcoholism and **drug** addiction. Then one day

Taking no chances: David Lynch with his top shirt button done up during the making of *Blue Velvet*. (BFI)

Mr Beaumont waters the lawn. (BFI)

The beginning of the mystery: Jeffrey discovers the ear. (BFI)

Dorothy at the Slow Club. Her stage act is just that – with the costume and the stage lights and the makeup – a pretence, a hiding-away from the pain of her real life. (Corbis/Everett)

The face that outraged a thousand critics: Dorothy likes to be hurt. (BFI)

The Angriest Dog in the World. (BFI)

ake-believe: Ben bewitches Frank with his rendering of 'In Dreams', a performance which is itself a kind
possession. He mouths the words to a cassette, but it's another person's voice, another person's song. (BFI)

The Morning After. (BFI)

Looking for wisdom. (Corbis/Everett)

Our first sight of Sandy is in a photograph in her father's study. In front of her portrait sits a wooden duc
a symbol of perfect proportion. (BFI)

Frank dressed to kill in a blood-red shirt and clutching his favourite blue-velvet gown.
(Corbis/Everett)

Jeffrey and Sandy enjoying a moment of domestic happiness after the nightmare. (BFI)

Hopper rang Lynch up himself and said, 'I must play Frank because I *am* Frank.' That, Lynch recalled later, nearly ended the matter once and for all, as just about the last thing he wanted to do was to work with Frank Booth. But he received reassurances that Hopper was on the wagon and discovered that there had been no problems in the recent films he'd appeared in.

Hopper himself would later explain that his drug addiction had brought him into the kind of circles that the drug dealer Frank would have inhabited. 'It wasn't so much that I was Frank Booth as that I'd seen Frank. I'd been with them, known them, they'd been friends. It was something I really understood.' His account of his own drug addiction can make Frank seem almost moderate by comparison: 'Most of the time I could drink half a gallon of rum a day, mixed with like fruit juices and stuff, 28 beers or so and do three grammes of cocaine to sober up and basically go through a working day without seeming that disorientated.'

If Hopper's personal life and his movie roles can seem to blur into each other, this was a natural part of his approach to acting. When he was 18 he was put under contract by Warner Brothers and appeared with James Dean in *Rebel Without a Cause*. He was so impressed with Dean's performance that he begged him to pass on the secret. 'You gotta do things and not show them,' Dean explained. 'You gotta drink the drink, not *act* drinking the drink. You gotta smoke the cigarette, not *act* smoking the cigarette. You gotta do simple reality. It'll be very difficult at first, but you'll get it.'

The difficulty that Dean had warned of came when Hopper got a small part in the Henry Hathaway film *From Hell to Texas*. Hopper was determined to put Dean's advice into practice and improvise, while the veteran Hollywood director was equally determined that the young actor should play the scene his way – as scripted. They fell out and Hopper repeatedly walked off the set. After eighty-six takes – according to Hopper – Hathaway eventually got the line reading he wanted and the actor was blacklisted by the studios.

Hopper went to New York to study the Method with Lee Strasberg and then spent most of the sixties guest-starring in television shows. But he made a spectacular comeback when he directed *Easy Rider* in 1969, which cost $420,000, and brought in $40,000,000.

The impression one has of Hopper in the late sixties is very much of a rebel *with* a cause. The success of *Easy Rider* broke the stranglehold of formulaic Hollywood cinema. Impressed by the huge returns of such a shoestring production, the studios were prepared, for a short while at least, to back a more intelligent kind of film-making. Riding high on the success of *Easy Rider*, Hopper went down to Peru to make a movie with a $1,000,000 of Universal's money. When he returned with an abstract expressionist film with a non-linear narrative, aptly named *The Last Movie*, he found himself effectively blacklisted for the second time in his career.

In its own way *Blue Velvet* was as notable a challenge to the values of the system in **the eighties** as *Easy Rider* had been in the sixties. It gained hugely from Hopper's iconic presence. It was as if the drugged disillusionment that separated the two decades had transformed the dope-smoking biker of *Easy Rider* into the monster Frank – as if he had joined the rednecks who had blown his partner off the road. The Easy Rider, taking the road of freedom to New Orleans, becomes the Joy Rider of *Blue Velvet*. When Frank takes Jeffrey on a 'joyride' it's a nightmare journey of brutality and compulsion. With these ghosts from the past Frank becomes a chilling subversion of a more innocent time – like the sixties songs he twists into anthems of death.

Hopper, the great Hollywood rebel, was born in the Wild West town of Dodge City, in Kansas – which Lynch, as an admirer of *The Wizard of Oz*, considered to be a good omen. Hopper had been raised on a small farm by his grandparents, who kept chickens, pigs and a few cows. It was pretty much the exact situation of the Judy Garland character Dorothy Gale in the film. Just as Dorothy Gale had wanted to escape somewhere over the rainbow, the young Hopper longed to get on the train that passed through the prairie once a day and escape to the world he saw in the movies. It may not have been something that an audience could possibly have realised, but at least in Lynch's own mind the association gave the relationship between Frank and Dorothy an enigmatic depth.

With Hopper's understanding of the character the evil Frank took on human characteristics – psychotic, deeply dangerous, but also someone for whom we can feel pity and, I think, even a kind of alarmed affection. Hopper knew some of the demons that drove Frank, had a sense too of how, although he was an extreme, the character represented a dark side that was an intrinsic part of humanity.

Frank is often cited as being one of the great villains of modern cinema, but he's really too much a victim himself to make a very convincing one, in the grip of something he cannot control. Hopper understood this vulnerability and the destructive effect that Frank's addictions have on him. Even in Frank's moments of most extreme evil, Hopper's performance brings out this vein of helplessness. After Frank has raped Dorothy in her apartment he shakes his arm violently in a series of involuntary spasms. When he discovers that Jeffrey, whom he thought he had just killed, has tricked him he blunders madly about Dorothy's apartment in a disoriented, childlike rage. We may will Jeffrey to slay this monster, but we still find a pathos in his benighted torment.

Hopper brought to the part of Frank an unreserved passion that obliterated the line between actor and character. The veins in his ravaged face bulging with anger and the fierceness in the cold, stony blue eyes seem to stem from some elemental force that he shares with Frank. You feel he's delivered what he promised in his telephone call: he *is* Frank.

With *Blue Velvet*, actor and character went their separate ways. Frank had his brains blown out, Hopper went on to enjoyed renewed success and stardom. He was the eponymous bigot in *Paris Trout*, a hitman in *Red Rock West*, the psychotic bomber Howard Payne in *Speed*, for which he won the MTV 'best villain' award, and the evil warlord Deacon – 'Don't just stand there, kill something!' – looking for land in *Waterworld*.

These were just a very few of the bad guy roles since *Blue Velvet*. Any movie producer in Hollywood looking for a convincing heavy today is likely to have Hopper on his list. Like Henry Hathaway wearing down the young actor to get the take he wanted, finally Tinseltown has persuaded the rebel to conform. Enjoying the renewed favour of the establishment, he even got the chance to direct again, with *Colors* – bringing a touch of realism to what would otherwise have been a routine cop movie – *The Hot Spot* and *Chasers*.

But the ghost of Frank was never far away. He lingers on in all those hoodlums and psychopaths, and has won a cherished place in movie-goers' memories, as well as being Hopper's own favourite villain. 'Since *Blue Velvet* a lot of guys and a *helluva* lot of women have approached me telling me how much they admire Frank. I keep hearing people whispering, "Don't you fuckin' look at me! Don't you fuckin' look at me!" It's kinda weird but I've grown to quite like it.'

Hopper, Edward (1882–1967)

Lynch has often spoken of his admiration for Edward Hopper's **paintings**. The two men have an important influence in common. In 1900 Hopper attended the New York School of Art, where he was taught by **Robert Henri**, whose book *The Art Spirit* would inspire Lynch many years later. 'You must not forget that I was for a time a student of Henri's who encouraged all his students to try to depict the familiar life about them,' wrote Hopper. Many scenes in *Blue Velvet* display the same sensitivity to **mood** and the emotional resonance of the ordinary, although with a surreal twist that makes them inimitably Lynch's own. The solitary fat man, for example, who stands statue-like in the **darkness** waiting for his little dog to pee. Jeffrey passes him on his way to see Detective Williams. It's such a fleeting moment, but captures the texture of **neighbourhood** life.

Lynch started out as an artist who wanted his paintings to move. Hopper's work gives one the same feeling. Take *High Noon*, for example, with its movie title name. A young woman stands at the front door of a clapboard house. Her dress is open and she holds a cigarette in one hand. The curtains in one of the dormer windows above are slightly apart, revealing the darkness of the room within. You can imagine the moments leading up to the scene – the woman walking through the house from her bedroom upstairs and opening the front door – and you want to know how it will continue. You wonder what's on the woman's mind. There are the traces of an unseen drama, a story to her open dress, and the curtains to the rooms above, one set half-open, the other shut. What's happening? Hopper's paintings may not have a third dimension, but they are strongly suggestive of the fourth. His canvases seem to have soaked up and frozen time, with all its sense of things about to happen – they are *suspense* pictures in the truest if less familiar sense of that phrase. 'Instantly, when you see those works, you dream,' Lynch has commented.

'So much of every art is an expression of the subconscious that it seems to me most of all of the important qualities are put there unconsciously, and little of importance by the conscious intellect.' Hopper wrote these words but it could have been Lynch speaking. If both Hopper's paintings and Lynch's films are fiercely **American** in subject matter, yet somehow feel unAmerican, I think it's because they share a degree of intuitive reflectiveness that one does not normally associate with the New World. Their instinct is to dwell and linger, while the pioneering spirit is to tell the story how it is and move on.

After art school Hopper travelled to Europe in 1906 to see the work of the great artists at first hand, as his teacher Robert Henri had encouraged him to. The first city he painted in any detail was not an American one, but Paris. For years after his return to New York the canvases he displayed were those painted during that trip. The American ones for which he is remembered came much later, and were a fusion of American themes and a sensibility that drew heavily on European influences. As late as 1962 Hopper insisted, 'I'm still an impressionist.'

The cinema does not provide such handy categories, but this pull of cultures seems equally true of Lynch. *Blue Velvet* created a familiar American landscape – in many respects it recalls Capra and Hitchcock – yet the strength of Lynch's personal vision places it more comfortably in a European tradition of auteurist cinema than Hollywood.

See **influences**.

horse's mouth, the

David Lynch does not like to talk about his work but has probably done so more than any other contemporary director. Last year, to coincide with the release of *Lost Highway*, an in-depth interview book, *Lynch on Lynch*, was published. It was based on a number of conversations he had had over a three-year period with the writer and film-maker Chris Rodley. More than 250 pages long, it appeared to be an extraordinary act of self-revelation for someone who supposedly had such a hatred of words.

It was an intriguing paradox. Lynch's first wife described his short film *The Alphabet* as being about 'the hell of a person with a non-verbal nature'. Yet here was the book, and the countless previous interviews, in which he explained himself very well – his good humour and affability even suggesting an eagerness to talk. Indeed, he seemed so forthcoming that at first I thought there was no point in joining the queue of interviewers that this apparent accessibility surely encouraged.

But the more I read, the more I got a sense of *déjà vu*; the more all these different interviews seem really to be just one interview. Talking to Chris Rodley about the importance of ideas, Lynch commented:

You've gotta be true to them because they're bigger than you first think they are. They're almost like gifts, and even if you don't understand them one hundred per cent, if you're true to them, they'll ring true at different levels. But if you alter them too much they won't even ring. They'll just sort of clank. I really believe it's like the Beach Boys said: 'Be true to your school.'

A decade earlier in an interview with *Film Comment*, Lynch said:

I really believe it's like the Beach Boys said: 'Be true to your school.' You gotta be true to the ideas that you have, because they're even bigger than you first think they are. And if you're not true to them, they'll only work part way. They're almost like gifts, and even if you don't understand them 100 percent, if you're true to them, they'll ring true at different levels and have truth at different levels. But if you alter them too much then they won't even ring. They'll just sorta clank.

This is Lynch in 1997 talking about sex in *Blue Velvet*:

Sex is such a fascinating thing. It's like jazz: you can listen to one pop song just so many times, whereas jazz has so many variations. Sex should be like that. It can be the same tune, but there are many variations on it. And then, when you start getting out there, it can be shocking to learn that something like that could be sexual. It would be kind of, you know, strange. But it's a real fact of life just the same. There's no real explaining it in *Blue Velvet* because it's just such an abstract thing in a person.

And this is Lynch in 1986:

> Sex is such a fascinating thing. It's sorta like you can listen to
> one pop song just so many times, whereas jazz has so many
> variations. Sex should be like jazz. It can be the same tune, but
> there are many variations on it. And then when you start getting
> out there, it can be shocking to learn that something like that
> could be sexual. It would be kind of, you know, strange. But
> it's a real fact of life just the same. There's no real explaining it
> in *Blue Velvet* because it's such an abstract thing inside a person.

As I read through all the repetitions I was reminded of Henry in
Eraserhead playing the same old gramophone record endlessly. It
occurred to me that the just as endless interviews were not so much
gateways to Lynch's thoughts as bulwarks, their purpose not to explain
but to fend off – to protect the inner sanctum.

Lynch spoke once – probably more than once – of his fear of
psychology. 'What it does is, it destroys the mystery, this kind of
magical quality. It can be reduced down to certain neuroses or certain
things, and since it's now named and defined, it's lost its mystery and
the potential for a vast, infinite experience.' For all his apparent
openness, the same fear underlies all the many interviews he has
given. They go only so far. He has discovered a way of saying a
lot while saying very little. There are vast, unexplained areas, but he
prefers that it should remain that way.

As I came to realise how many questions remained unanswered, I
decided that I should try to talk to him. I faxed him via his agent, left
messages on the agent's answerphone. But my efforts became increasingly half-hearted. Eventually I came to fear the contact I was seeking,
even to view it as an intrusion – like Jeffrey venturing into **Deep
River Apartments**. In any case, I consoled myself, the well-worn
Lynch needle would just slip into the old groove. I imagined trying

to remain attentive, as he told me that you've gotta be true to your ideas, that if you alter them too much they won't even ring, they'll just sorta clank.

Lynch was right. Sometimes it's better to work out things for yourself.

Hunter

The blond, silent member of Frank's **gang**, played by J. Michael Hunter.

I

influences

There's something one-off about David Lynch and something unmediated about his vision. It is an index of his uniqueness that he has cited his biggest influence as being not a book or a film or a person, but a place – **Philadelphia**. He is so outside any tradition that attempts to classify him are more misleading than helpful. Many commentators have labelled *Blue Velvet* 'surrealist'. But if Lynch's work does have a surreal aspect it is less a conscious borrowing from the surrealists than a coincidental – and partial – affinity in the way he views the world. As Pauline Kael observed, *Blue Velvet* is 'an anomaly – the work of a genius naif'.

As far as films are concerned, *Blue Velvet* owes its greatest debt to such American classics as ***Rear Window, It's a Wonderful Life*** and ***The Wizard of Oz***. But they are reference points rather than a tradition to which the film belongs – raw material which Lynch manipulates for his own very different purpose.

Although Lynch has spoken of his admiration for such people as Kafka, **Francis Bacon** and **Edward Hopper**, it seems to me best to think of them more as kindred spirits than influences. Recently the production designer on *Blue Velvet* and Lynch's regular collaborator Patricia Norris built a set modelled closely on Hopper's **painting** *Nighthawks* for Wim Wenders' film *The End of Violence*. 'Edward Hopper has been a continuous inspiration to me and to many other film-makers,' Wenders would comment. 'When the necessity came up to actually construct a diner set, I thought of turning that into an outspoken homage.' Such homage has become the passion of the postmodern age, whether in Wenders' work or Tarantino's, but it's alien to the organic nature of Lynch's cinema, which draws its power from a directness of observation and relies more on intuition than intellect.

See **Henri, Robert**; **Shostakovitch**.

It's a Wonderful Life

Lynch's **Lumberton** reminds me of another small town called Bedford Falls – the folksy near-Utopia of Frank Capra's 1946 film with **James Stewart** and Donna Reed. As just about every man, woman and child knows, George Bailey longed to get away from it but never did, always in the end sacrificing his ambitions for other people. Like *The Wizard of Oz*, that other film whose spirit *Blue Velvet* draws on so heavily, *It's a Wonderful Life* has become a treasured part of **Americana**, articulating the way a nation would like to see itself. Every Christmas it's on television, and, if anything, as the years pass it gets only more poignant. Not just because the modern world seems so much more like Pottersville, the hard town that Bedford Falls would have become without George Bailey, but because its vision of communal goodness is so difficult to live up to in real life.

George Bailey. Jeffrey Beaumont. On the surface they're very alike. Each stays at home to look after the family business when his father has a stroke. For George, who had hoped to travel the world and go to college, it's a terrible narrowing of his horizons, but he sacrifices his ambitions with a sense of duty not only to his family but to the town – his family's business, the Bailey Building and Loan, is the only place where citizens can get a fair mortgage for their home. We never question George Bailey's goodness for a single moment –

indeed, the whole film is contrived to show it off. It is there right at the beginning when at the age of 12 he pulls his younger brother out of a frozen pond, losing his hearing in one ear in the process; with one sacrifice after another he goes on to prove his goodness over and over again. He may suffer a crisis of confidence in his adulthood and need the reassurance of a guardian angel that he still matters, but as a character he is fully formed, his spiritual development complete. If George's world is a limited one, this is as much a result of his own character as any lack of opportunity. It is his sense of duty that makes him choose to thwart his curiosity.

For Jeffrey, coming home is the opening of a world, not the closing of one. While George simply steps into the shoes of his father, Jeffrey, in the absence of his, enjoys a freedom to embark on his own path of self-discovery. He's a less immediately attractive character than the lovable George Bailey, but more realistically drawn. While George's character is predetermined, Jeffrey's is fluid and responsive to circumstances. He's not obviously *good* the way George is, but along the way he learns some of the lessons to understand what goodness might involve.

There are no mysteries in *It's a Wonderful Life*, nothing that the audience has to figure out for itself. We meet George's future wife, Mary, for the first time when she is only 9 years old. Young George is serving in Mr Gower's drugstore. As he stoops to get Mary a soda, she whispers into his bad ear, 'Is this the ear you can't hear on? George Bailey, I'll love you till the day I die.' From this moment their eventual union is not a question of if, only of when, and 'happily ever after' is assured. When we next meet Mary, at 18, she has acquired a soft-focus aura – the Hollywood equivalent of the Madonna's halo, to add to her name. She and George walk home from a high-school reunion party through the night-time streets of Bedford Falls. It's a courtship of harmless japes and heartfelt speeches. 'What is it you want, Mary? What do you want? You want the moon? Just say the word and I'll throw a lassoo round it and pull it down. Hey, that's a pretty good idea, I'll give you the moon, Mary.' Just thinking of this scene easily brings a lump to my throat. We long for things to be so simple and pure but know that they rarely are. It's a film of wishful thinking. It tells us that angels really do exist, and that good people do bad things only when driven to it by evil men like Mr Potter.

Jeffrey and Sandy also walk through the night-time streets of their town, and they too are engaged in a courtship of sorts, but it is on the sly. Their lives are so much more confused and uncertain. Sandy already has a boyfriend, whom she says she loves, but will soon ditch for Jeffrey. And Jeffrey's attraction to Sandy does not stop him from exploring the dark world of **Deep River Apartments**.

Jeffrey becomes enfatuated with Dorothy and two-times Sandy. It's impossible to imagine such conduct from the hero of Bedford Falls. Such are the tramlines of character that we know he will never succumb to temptation. Indeed, he rejects the advances of the town flirt, pretty Violette Bick. With Jeffrey you feel that anything could happen, as anything can happen in real life. But poor George is chaperoned by his scriptwriters. In the land of Capracorn, heroes must – in the essentials at least – be spotless, and the villains beyond redemption.

Blue Velvet may portray a morally messy world, but it is an infinitely more human one. Lynch manages to elicit some feeling even for a monster like Frank, but Capra requires us only to hiss at Mr Potter.

To stop him from committing suicide, George's guardian angel shows him what would have happened if he had never been born. Gentle Bedford Falls becomes the nightmarish Pottersville, a town where the barmen 'serve hard drinks for men who want to get drunk fast'. This notion that good and bad are somehow mutually exclusive is the key to the difference between the films. In *Blue Velvet* Bedford Falls and Pottersville exist together in the same town, just as good and bad exist in every individual.

J

Jeffrey

Until the severed **ear** turned up he had nothing better to do than work in his parents' hardware store and toss stones at bottles. He is bored by the dullness of home, where the bland formulaic images of television hold his mother and Aunt Barbara in a sleepy obeisance. There is nothing to keep Jeffrey at home, and it's no surprise, given the lack of stimulus of his home life, that he should be so excited about the ear he's found. He's so curious about what it means that on the evening of the day he finds it, after already having seen Detective Williams in his office, he visits him again at home. Detective Williams warns him not to get involved. But later he learns of the mysterious Dorothy Vallens and the chance to unravel the secrets of the severed ear becomes too enticing to resist.

What makes Jeffrey different from the merely curious are the extreme lengths he's prepared to go to in order to discover things. When Sandy warns him that sneaking into Dorothy's apartment is 'crazy and dangerous', far from making him have second thoughts this seems only to encourage him. Part of the appeal of what he does is its danger – although this is before he knows what the danger really amounts to. His curiosity is an obsessive, self-generating drive. Jeffrey looking and Jeffrey hearing are stressed throughout the film. We see his eyes again and again in close-up – watching his father in hospital, looking at Dorothy and Frank through the slit of Dorothy's **closet,** looking at Frank's hideout with his camera in a shoebox, looking at the door where Dorothy's son is kept hostage, and so on.

Jeffrey has that all-consuming appetite, both bodily and spiritual, of the young on the verge of adulthood, whether for knowledge or adventure or **sex** or love. 'Are you hungry or thirsty or both?' he asks Sandy as he picks her up to take her to **Arlene's** diner. Even when an angry Frank tells Jeffrey not to look at him, his eyes, momentarily averted, quickly wander back. For all its foolhardiness, we cannot fail to admire his bravery. There's a determination to fathom his situation regardless of the danger. It's the basis of his moral strength. He recognises evil and is prepared to respond to it. When Frank molests Dorothy in the car, Jeffrey tells him to leave her alone, punching him in the face when he refuses.

But in many ways Jeffrey is – as Frank might put it – a bit of a shithead. He may be well meaning, but it is a prurient fascination that spurs him on. In his general pursuit of experience he is careless of moral consequences. Dorothy's obvious mental distress and the discovery that she is a married woman with a husband do not deter him from exploiting the opportunity for sexual adventure that she offers. He takes full advantage of her misfortune. The fact that her husband is a hostage in the hands of a dangerous psychopath may be shocking news to Jeffrey, but it is also a bit of good luck – a rival is safely out of the way.

Jeffrey keeps Sandy abreast of what he is discovering, but only what it suits him to tell her. She hears about the kidnaps and about Frank, but nothing about Dorothy discovering him in the closet, and certainly nothing about the sexual adventures that follow. On the basis of what he does, Jeffrey is a deceitful two-timer. There's something flagrant about it. We see him stealing a kiss from Sandy in one scene, and embracing Dorothy passionately in the next. We just don't notice because he's so disarming. We respond to his charm and his all-**American** good looks. He's a lesson in what handsome, plausible people can get away with – like **Lumberton** itself, a handsome exterior hides a darker soul.

Jeffrey is as much taken in by his own image as everyone else. With such obvious villains as Frank about, it is easy for him to imagine that somehow he is on the right side. It takes the practised victim Dorothy to teach him that he too is capable of evil. When Dorothy asks Jeffrey to hit her, at first he resists, then, as if in his very anger at her continued insistence, finally he obliges. This anger then turns into a savage pleasure as he and Dorothy have sex with bestial abandon. Jeffrey ends up taking pleasure out of the very last thing he could have imagined himself wanting to do. It's an extraordinary scene of twists and paradoxes. Dorothy is the victim but also the victor. Her triumph is to expose Jeffrey's frailty. 'I have your disease in me now,' she says quietly afterwards with contentment in her voice.

Though Jeffrey's visits to **Deep River Apartments** may mark his fall from grace, he is redeemed by his sense of shame. When he looks back on his conduct with Dorothy the next day, his remorse is genuine. In a scene which for me has all the power of Masaccio's **painting** of Adam and Eve being banished from the Garden of Eden, he weeps inconsolably as he recalls losing control and striking Dorothy. He has discovered some awful truths about himself, but in doing so has made some spiritual progress.

But there's a sadness too about Jeffrey's getting of wisdom. One of the lessons he has learnt is not to mix with people like Dorothy. Even as he takes his leave of her, promising to call her soon, he seems ready to let her down. 'Are you lying to me?' asks Dorothy, sensing the reluctance in his tone, and we know now that he has no further reason to remain with her.

K

Kafka, Franz (1883–1924)

See **influences**.

L

Lange, Hope (b. 1933)

When Sandy and Jeffrey arrive on her doorstep with a naked and mad Dorothy, Mrs Williams deals with the situation with the composure of someone who has seen it all before. This is what life can be like if you're married to a cop. The casting of Hope Lange as Mrs Williams had a providential aptness. A respectable mother in *Blue Velvet*, Lange had a generation earlier, in 1957, played an abused daughter in the film version of **Peyton Place**. She won an **Oscar** nomination for her role as Selina Cross. Raped and impregnated by her stepfather, the caretaker of the high school, Selina is put on trial after accidentally killing him. The small **American** town of Peyton Place, outwardly innocent, had as many dark secrets as Lynch's **Lumberton**.

Born in 1933, Lange made her film debut in *Bus Stop*. Other film appearances include *The True Story of Jesse James*, *A Pocketful of Miracles*, *How the West was Won* and *Death Wish*. She won an Emmy Award for her performance in the TV series *The Ghost and Mrs Muir*.

love stories

Dennis Hopper described Frank as 'one of the great romantic leads of all time'. Frank is a man so much in love that he will do anything. To hold on to Dorothy, he'll kidnap her son, and cut off her husband's **ear**. Eventually he'll kill the husband and try to kill Jeffrey too, his rival for her love. It is a diseased and twisted love that can express itself only in violence. But characters like Frank have existed probably since the dawn of time. Thinking about him brought to mind this Latin poem I knew at school and had long forgotten: '*Odi et amo; quare id faciam, fortasse requiris/nescio, sed fieri sentio et excrucior*' – 'I love and I hate. Why do I do this you might ask? I don't know, but it hurts' – Catullus, about 50 BC. The ancients understood far better than our sanitised generation how close love and hate can be. In Frank the two have come together so that they are indistinguishable. He loves and he hates in one motion. He weeps over a piece of blue velvet as Dorothy sings the song in **the Slow Club**; he wraps it around his gun as he hunts Jeffrey down. Killing for him is a sexual act.

The night he beats Jeffrey up after the joyride, it's as much a love scene. Frank's no ordinary two-bit thug, he's a man in the grip of a grand passion. He doesn't just lay into Jeffrey, he smothers him with kisses, although you feel he could equally well bite out his tongue. 'Don't be a good neighbor to her or I'm gonna send you a love letter straight from my heart, fucker.' His tone is as much pleading as threatening. It's a warning to Jeffrey to leave Dorothy alone, but it's also mixed in with a kind of fellow feeling. Through Dorothy their lives have come together.

Dorothy in turn loves Frank, however perverse and self-destructive it may be to do so. One thing Frank cannot be accused of is indifference. He's a passionate lover who shows total commitment. He may hit her and abuse her, but he makes her feel that she is the most important person in his world. They have a shared bond in their vulnerability, and their need to love without reserve.

In his constancy Frank puts Jeffrey to shame. Jeffrey's love for Dorothy is an infatuation. He doesn't know where it's going to go, just as he confesses to Sandy that he doesn't know where his investigation is going, but the logic of such inquisitive love is that, like the investigation, it will come to an end. For the most important thing is that he's finding out things. Jeffrey uses Dorothy, then drops her. When she turns up naked on his doorstep he would disown her if he could. Physical violence is always more dramatic, but this brush-off has its own cruelty. She becomes just some mad woman off the street, who can be only an embarrassment in his world. Even Frank never made her feel of so little account. The scene in which she is taken to the Williams's house is chilling. Awkward in front of Sandy and her mother, Jeffrey is stiff and cold. 'I LOVE YOU,' Dorothy shouts at him. 'LOVE ME!' It's a heart-rending reproach from someone who has given without limit.

The world of Frank and Dorothy, into which Jeffrey briefly intrudes, feeds on unchecked emotions. It is shrouded in darkness. It is unsustainable, and self-destruction is its natural end. It's a kind of *amour fou* which in its disorder and un-reason is at an opposite pole from the kind of love that Jeffrey and Sandy seem to be heading for. When they acknowledge their love for each other at the party, it is a moment of harmony and balance.

In *Blue Velvet* there are two overlapping love triangles, in which Jeffrey is the common element: Frank, Dorothy and Jeffrey; Jeffrey, Sandy and Mike. The one faintly echoes the other. Frank warns Jeffrey to stay away from Dorothy and then beats him up in **Meadow Lane**. After it has become obvious that Jeffrey has stolen Sandy's affections, Mike chases the two in his car and forces a showdown outside Jeffrey's house. Like Frank, he's got his gang of beer-drinking mates with him. But the intervention of a naked and deranged Dorothy saves Jeffrey from a second beating. Her presence is so alien that it stops Mike in his tracks. It's an index of how mutually exclusive these different worlds are. It was only Jeffrey's unrestrained curiosity that enabled him to move between the two.

Jeffrey is as much Sandy's 'secret lover' as Jeffrey is Dorothy's. The difference is that, while Jeffrey wants to have love both sacred and profane, Sandy is searching only for the first kind.

Lumberton

The imaginary town where *Blue Velvet* takes place.

See **Wilmington**.

Lynch, David (b. 1946)

Once upon a time, deep in the forest there lived a forest-keeper and his wife. They had a son, whom they called David . . .

It wasn't quite like this, but almost. David Lynch's father was a research scientist who worked for the Forest Service, and his mother stayed at home to bring up David and his younger brother and sister. They lived not in one forest, but in several all over **America**. He was born in Missoula, Montana, in 1946, and the list of the childhood moves that followed reads like a sketch for a future Lynch road movie: Sandpoint, Idaho; Spokane, Washington; Durham, North Carolina; Boise, Idaho, finally settling in Alexandria, Virginia, where he went to high school.

But wherever he was in his early years, the forest provided a continuum, and Lynch's descriptions of his childhood make clear the lasting impression the forest had on him.

> My father . . . would drive me through the woods in his green Forest Service truck, over dirt roads, through the most beautiful forests where the trees are very tall and shafts of sunlight come down, and in the mountain streams the rainbow trout leap out and their little trout sides catch glimpses of light. Then my father would drop me in the woods and go off. It was a weird, comforting feeling being in the woods. There were odd, mysterious things. That's the kind of world I grew up in.

Watching *Blue Velvet*, you feel that Lynch the child is very much present. In the opening shots the roses and tulips are seen from a low angle, as if by a child lying in the grass; and the fireman on the running board of the fire engine seems to be waving to a child. While for most of us our senses become dulled with age, Lynch rekindles with ease the intensity of a young person's perception. 'I feel between nine and seventeen most of the time,' he has commented, 'and sometimes around six!' His films can evoke a powerful nostalgia for those childhood years, because they recreate the way they felt with such fidelity.

As a child Lynch drew all the time, and he has often cited his mother's refusal to give him colouring books as a key to his creative development. 'Once you have that colouring book, the whole idea is to stay between the lines.' The remark reminds me of John Merrick, in Lynch's *The Elephant Man*, building from his imagination a splendid model of a church when from his hospital room all he could see above the rooftops was the steeple.

Lynch remembers his childhood as blissfully happy: 'elegant homes, tree-lined streets, the milkman, building backyard forts, droning airplanes, blue skies, picket fences, green grass, cherry trees. Middle America as it's supposed to be.' Yet at the same time, wandering in those forests he was more than usually aware for a person of his age of the death and decay of the natural world. The contrast between his own security and his awareness of an external chaos would have sewn seeds of anxiety. *Blue Velvet* is the work of someone who has known mostly good fortune in his life but fears it will be snatched away.

After the forests and small towns of his childhood, visits to New York City, where his grandparents lived, provided him with another stark contrast. 'Going into the subway, I felt, I was really going down into hell,' Lynch would recall. 'It was the total fear of the unknown: the wind from those trains, the sounds, the smells and the different light and mood that was really special in a traumatic way.' He remembered too his grandfather unscrewing his car aerial every night so that gangs wouldn't break it off. 'I could just *feel* fear in the air.'

Reading Lynch's reminiscences of his childhood, one is left with the impression that there was no single, searing event that marked the future film-maker like Hitchcock supposedly being slung into a prison cell, but, instead, a deepening impression over time of an endemic chaos. Lynch – as Hitchcock had done – specialises in the cinema of anxiety, but relies on **mood** rather than suspense. While Hitchcock's films anticipate some dire threat to a fundamentally ordered world, Lynch's expose such order as a chimera.

Lynch seems to have regarded high school as a place that shut you up in a room all day and stopped you learning: 'The things that you're asked to do are not inspiring, and more often than not, it restricts people. And pretty soon this thing in your brain that is free, and could evolve, gets clamped shut and you can't move any more.' You can find the traces of his attitude in *Blue Velvet*, when Jeffrey asks Sandy about **Central**, the high school he's left and which she still attends. It's 'terrible' and 'boring', she confides. 'What else is new?' he replies. Jeffrey has to leave college to discover the really interesting things.

A more overt autobiographical touch was left out of the film. While at school, Lynch had run for the office of class treasurer under the slogan 'Save with Dave' and lost. Referring to Jeffrey's time at the school, Sandy says in the script, 'You were pretty popular. Didn't you run for some office?' And Jeffrey replies, 'Yeah I did. Treasurer.'

The most significant developments for the young Lynch were extracurricular. His passion had always been **painting**, but living out in the north-west he didn't think it was something you could do for real. But in Virginia he made a friend, Toby Keeler, who told him that his father was a painter. He visited Bushnell Keeler's studio in Georgetown, became friends and decided that he would be a painter. While he was still at high school he rented a studio with a friend, Jack Fisk. He also attended a Saturday class at the Corcoran School of Art in Washington, DC. After high school he studied art at the Boston Museum School, but was unhappy there and abandoned the course after a year. The months that followed were a low point for Lynch. A planned three-year trip to Europe to study painting was abandoned after only two weeks, and he returned to Virginia. His parents refused to support him unless he went to college, and he drifted through a series of jobs, getting fired several times for lateness.

Lynch remembers that he was miserable, and this period of his life seems to have been the closest that he came to going off the rails. Such periods of non-achievement tend to be passed over in the newspaper profiles, but he would later achieve such striking portraits of stagnation and helplessness in characters like Henry in *Eraserhead* or Dorothy in *Blue Velvet* that one feels that it must have been a fertile time for him even if it did not seem so then. It would have been interesting to see the young Lynch turn up to one of those jobs.

Going off the rails – or being driven off them – is a theme in Lynch's films: Sailor in *Wild at Heart* getting talked into a bank robbery, Laura Palmer in *Twin Peaks* getting mixed up in things she shouldn't, John Merrick the Elephant Man being spirited away from his sanctuary and forced to work in a freak show, and Dorothy's husband and son being kidnapped in *Blue Velvet*. There's a strong sense of people's vulnerability and their need for guidance in a confusing world. In *Wild at Heart*, when Sailor gets out of gaol he hesitates to return to Lula and their young son. He feels that with his own lack of 'parental guidance' he will not make a good enough father. But in a **fairy tale** happy ending a Good Witch visits him and tells him that if he's really wild at heart he should fight for his dreams.

In *Blue Velvet* Jeffrey gets into trouble by ignoring advice – Detective Williams tells him not to get involved in the investigation and Sandy warns him more than once not to sneak into Dorothy's apartment. In one of the very first images of the film, the crossing attendant guides the small **children** across the road. Sandy benefits from the protective presence of her parents, just as Jeffrey only wanders into danger once his father has been struck down.

Lynch's own appreciation of the support of both parents and friends is made very clear in his interviews. At key moments they helped him to become the artist he wanted to be. Just as his mother made a crucial contribution by keeping him away from colouring books, his father paid half the rent of the studio he hired while still at school – 'a super-cool thing for my father to do, because having a studio was not a normal thing'. When Lynch finally ended his slouching around in Virginia and decided to go to college again, it was partly due to the behind-the-scenes activity of other people. 'Bushnell Keeler and my father and a couple of painters in the area were all conspiring to make life miserable for me,' he explained. 'I used to be able to go over and have a coffee with Bushnell and, you know, talk. But then he started telling me he was too busy and for me to get out, and stuff like this. And it was all to try to get me to go to art school and get it together.' Then a friend, who had just gone to the Pennsylvania Academy of Fine Art in **Philadelphia**, told him what a wonderful time he was having there, and Lynch made a successful application to the college.

Lynch didn't think he would have gone if people had tried to persuade him to do so directly. 'At that age you're in a very rebellious frame of mind. And I think you've got to be tricked.' In *Blue Velvet*, at first Jeffrey disregards the advice of his elders, but as he realises the extent of the trouble he's got himself into he has a change of heart. It's a lesson he has to learn for himself.

'I never wanted to go to Philadelphia,' commented Lynch. 'I always wanted to go to Boston. Philadelphia was horrible – full of fear and crime and decay. But this atmosphere was so strong, and so magical, that your imagination was always sparking in Philadelphia.' As Lynch habitually cites the city as the biggest influence in his life, perhaps one of the lessons it taught him was that bad experiences can be good for you. At the end of *Wild at Heart* Sailor is beaten senseless by a street **gang**. It is then that he has a vision of the Good Witch. When he comes to, he thanks the gang. 'You taught me a valuable lesson in life.' In *Blue Velvet* Jeffrey's journey into darkness is also an opportunity 'for gaining knowledge and experience'. He tells Sandy: 'I'm seeing something that was always hidden. I'm involved in a mystery. I'm learning.' **Deep River Apartments** turns out to be Jeffrey's Philadelphia.

When Lynch first used film as an art student, it was less a revolutionary switch than an incorporation of a new element. He bought a 16 mm camera, and animated a painting of six heads into a minute-long film. There would be a fire and then each of the six heads would be sick. But this was just one element of the overall artwork. He got a friend to make a cast of him in plaster and put together three figures of himself to make a sculptured screen. The film, which was on a loop, was projected on to the screen and accompanied by a tape recording of a siren, which also played continuously on a loop. 'It was a painting and a sculpture show, but I had a film.'

The exhibit shared first prize at the Academy's end-of-the-year show. The great thing about art school for Lynch must have been the freedom to cross the conventional boundaries without anyone getting confused. *Six Men Getting Sick* was neither one thing or another, or perhaps both one thing and another and yet still another. An animation of his own painting projected on to a triple-image screen of himself, it was the epitome of the personal film – Lynch's face in triplicate merging with the picture like a watermark in a bank note. There was perhaps no more perfect symbol of the kind of cinema that, with one or two deviations, Lynch has practised ever since – a stark representation of his Protean view of things always being or becoming something else.

The necessary compromise Lynch had to make for the world to have a chance of eventually getting to know him was moving from the kind of installation art that *Six Men Getting Sick* represented to making a conventional film in the sense that he could leave a reel with a projectionist, go home and not worry. The four-minute film *The Alphabet* was a mixture of live action and animation which depicted a little girl's nightmare about learning the alphabet. It helped him win a grant from the American Film Institute (AFI), and with AFI money he went on to make *The Grandmother* in 1970. A boy is beaten by his parents for wetting his bed. He takes refuge in his room, where out of the damp patch in his bed he nurtures a pod that gives birth to an old woman. She provides him with the kindness and love his parents withheld. But soon the grandmother falls ill and dies. In despair, the boy retreats to his room and turns into a plant himself. Both these early films displayed a concern for nurture, or its absence, and the trials of growing up, which would become prominent themes in *Blue Velvet*.

The Grandmother helped Lynch gain admittance to the AFI's Advanced Film Center in Los Angeles, where he worked on a script that eventually became *Eraserhead*. Made on and off over a period of five years, it was a work of mood rather than narrative, in which Lynch's own life and Henry's would partially merge. As Henry's wife left him, so Lynch was divorced from his during the film's making, and he surreptitiously took up residence in the makeshift studios where the film was shot: 'I lived on the set, and in my mind I lived in that world. And the sets, the lighting, the mood of it helped. And since it took so much time, I really sank into it.'

This was the period of Bob's Big Boy. Every afternoon for seven years, from 1973 to 1979, Lynch would go to the same diner in Los Angeles and order the same chocolate milkshake and coffee. One has an impression of it being another womb for him, like the set of *Eraserhead*, a place of security where nothing untoward would happen. But it was also the place from which he could contemplate possible disorder, just as it is in the safety of Arlene's diner that his **alter ego** Jeffrey discusses his plans to sneak into Dorothy's apartment. 'I like to hang on to daydreams,' Lynch explained. 'But there must be optimum circumstances. I must sit in a bright illuminated room in which there's perfect order. For example a diner. There I let my mind travel. There I dare to enter fantastic worlds. And if I feel suddenly uneasy, I can immediately return to my diner.'

If in *Eraserhead* Lynch seemed partly to be hiding away, in *Blue Velvet* he confronted this struggle between chaos and order, with all its paradoxes, head on. The thirst for knowledge stems from an instinct to control – scientists set up experiments, artists paint pictures to get some kind of a handle on the world – yet this knowledge reveals only how beyond control the world is. Jeffrey's curiosity brings him face to face with his irrational side. Frightened by what he discovers, like David Lynch taking refuge in the safety of his diner, Jeffrey falls back on the certainties of home.

The affinity between the two films is so strong that it's no surprise to learn that even during the many years it took to make *Eraserhead* Lynch had often talked about *Blue Velvet*. Jack Nance (who played Henry) remembers visiting Lynch one day when he was editing the film.

> He showed me this little drawing he'd done . . . of this rustic roadhouse or saloon, out in the countryside. It was just by the side of the road with this big neon sign on top of the place that said: 'Blue Velvet.' He showed it to me and said: 'How do you like it, Jack?' I said: 'It's beautiful.' He said: 'We're going to do that someday.' I said: 'Do what?' And he said: 'We're going to do *Blue Velvet* someday. It's a movie.' When we were shooting that scene years later in that Roadhouse – when Hopper is sitting there fondling the blue velvet and Isabella is singing the song, it was incredible. After that first take I went over to David and said: 'I know how many years you've been waiting to hear that song.'

Few paths could have been more unlikely than the one that led to that moment in **the Slow Club**. The project Lynch would have liked to have made after *Eraserhead* was *Ronnie Rocket*, about a three-and-a-half-foot man with red hair and 'the absurd mystery of the strange forces of existence'. Not surprisingly, no studio was interested, and with such ideas Lynch was really painting himself into a corner of low-budget movie-making. *Eraserhead* itself was the sort of calling card to make most producers in Hollywood barricade the door, alien to everything they stood for. When Lynch was trying to get help to release the film, one potential backer exclaimed: 'PEOPLE DON'T ACT LIKE THAT! PEOPLE DON'T TALK LIKE THAT! THIS IS BULLSHIT!'

So it was something of a fluke when Stuart Cornfeld, a producer working for Mel Brooks, saw it on the late night circuit and thought it the greatest thing he had ever seen. Having finally given up hope of getting *Ronnie Rocket* off the ground, Lynch asked Cornfeld to look out for some suitable scripts for him, and by another fluke – or perhaps fate – Cornfeld came up with something that suited him perfectly. He suggested *The Elephant Man*, one of the projects that Mel Brooks's new company, Brooksfilms, had in development. Much to Lynch's surprise, Brooks loved *Eraserhead* too, supported the idea of him as director and, in spite of his inexperience, managed to secure the backing of a major studio.

The Elephant Man won eight **Oscar** nominations, including Best Director. Lynch was now hot. He tried once again, unsuccessfully, to get people interested in *Ronnie Rocket*. Richard Roth, one of the producers who had read it, asked him if he had any other scripts, and Lynch told him about his idea for *Blue Velvet*. They took it to Warner Brothers, who were interested. Lynch then wrote a script but Warner Brothers hated it and the project was back on the shelf again. Meanwhile George Lucas offered him the opportunity to direct the third *Star Wars* film, *The Return of the Jedi*, which he turned down because he disliked science fiction and thought he would have had little freedom within the framework of the series that Lucas had already established.

Lynch's mixed fortunes in the wake of *The Elephant Man* must have hammered home the message that being a successful director in Hollywood usually meant making films for other people. But *The Elephant Man* had been a positive experience in which he had been free to make the film as he had wanted. So it's easy to understand why he was prepared to accept another assignment.

Dino De Laurentiis asked him to read Frank Herbert's **Dune**, and this time, although it too was science fiction, he accepted. It seems a surprising decision, but it's easy to understand how Lynch's love of texture and atmosphere would have drawn him to a story which had at its heart a waterless desert planet and a strange mutant substance called spice: 'I thought about waves – water waves, sand waves, wave motions, symbols, repetition of shapes, connecting threads.' It was a chance to create another world – as he had with the nightmare landscape of *Eraserhead* and the Victorian London of *The Elephant Man*. But he was also interested in the central figure of Paul Atreides, 'the sleeper who must awaken and become what he is supposed to become'. This description of Atreides anticipated the character of Jeffrey in *Blue Velvet*, but also summed up the experience that making *Dune* would prove to be for Lynch himself – it decided the kind of film-maker he was to become.

His contract required him to produce a film that was not longer than 2 hours 17 minutes. As his control over mood and atmosphere depended on a leisurely pace, he found it impossible to pursue his own vision and yet still remain true to the complex narrative of the story. The producers, Raffaella and Dino De Laurentiis, also made it very clear what kind of film they expected. As Lynch did not have the right of final cut, 'little by little every decision was always made with them in mind and their sort of film'. It was a process in which he felt he had sold out.

The resulting compromise was a science-fiction epic of extraordinary incoherence. The frustration of failing to fathom the complex plot made it hard for the audience to appreciate the film's mainly visual merits. Perhaps it would have been better if Lynch had been able, as he put it, 'to make it more like a long poem. Just let it be abstract in some places, with no dialogue, and let it be a mood.' But the $50 million of the film's budget were against him.

The *Dune* experience taught him henceforward always to be true to his own vision. 'I was making it for the producers,' he commented, 'not for myself. That's why the right of final cut is crucial. One person has to be the filter for everything. I believe this is a lesson world; we're supposed to learn stuff. But 3½ years to learn that lesson is too long.'

Perhaps it's because Lynch's own account of working on *Dune* sounds so much like a cautionary tale that the parallels with *Blue Velvet* seem irresistible. Consumed with curiosity, he finds himself pulled into the strange world of big-budget movie-making. Its very difference from his previous work entices him. There's a degree of perversity since he doesn't even like science fiction. But he can see endless possibilities and there's the satisfaction of not quite knowing how it will turn out. He's in the middle of a mystery and he's learning. But then things get out of hand. Under the influence of the producers, he finds himself doing things which are contrary to his most precious beliefs about making films. He even savagely cuts the film he loves. He feels ashamed of himself, that he's sold out, and he resolves never to get involved in that kind of film-making again.

If agreeing to direct *Dune* was a bit like Jeffrey getting involved with Dorothy, then Lynch's resolve never again to venture away from personal film-making was the equivalent of Jeffrey coming home again. He had discovered the dangers of the glamorous world which had briefly seduced him and learnt to appreciate the familiar one he had left behind.

'It's a strange world,' goes the refrain in *Blue Velvet*. After Lynch had directed one of the great flops of modern cinema, Dino De Laurentiis nonetheless gave him the go-ahead to make *Blue Velvet*. He was even given artistic control on condition that he cut his salary and budget in half. It was a surprisingly enlightened attitude which would only have strengthened Lynch's belief in **providence** and life's contradictory nature. Like Philadelphia, the *Dune* experience had been horrible but positive too.

De Laurentiis bought the rights back from Warner Brothers, and Lynch set about writing another script. After the obvious narrative failure of *Dune*, perhaps Lynch was more concerned than he otherwise might have been that his next film should be accessible. Lynch has called *Blue Velvet* his most normal film. 'It's an American picture. It deals with human beings and human problems, and it's the present day and there are cars in the picture.' According to the cinematographer **Frederick Elmes**, who had worked with Lynch on *Eraserhead* and had discussed with him the look of *Blue Velvet* even before *Dune*, 'Lynch learned a lot on *Dune* in terms of story and writing and he was able to use that when rewriting *Blue Velvet*. So the story evolved and I think our vision changed.'

M

MacLachlan, Kyle (b. 1959)

In the opening scenes of *Blue Velvet* Jeffrey wears an open-necked shirt. But after he embarks upon unravelling the mystery of the severed **ear** he buttons the shirt up to the top, as if for extra protection from the dangers he is about to encounter. In this detail MacLachlan modelled his character on David Lynch, who has explained his habit of buttoned-up shirts as an 'insecurity thing'. Jeffrey, with his fascination for seeing things that were always hidden before, is obviously to an extent Lynch's **alter ego**, although one of the reasons why the character works so well is that he is also an Everyman figure with whom the whole audience can identify.

MacLachlan developed his love of drama when reading the *Hardy Boys* adventures as a child, acting out all the roles as he went along. He could not have known it at the time, but this was a perfect preparation for playing Jeffrey, the amateur detective.

While his co-star Laura Dern was born into an acting family and already a seasoned professional, MacLachlan was pretty much picked off Main Street, USA. The son of a stockbroker, he was born and raised in Yakima, Washington. He enrolled at the University of Washington in liberal arts, but switched to its theatre-arts programme after playing the lead role in a summer stock adaptation of Thomas Wolfe's *Homeward Angel*. After graduation in 1982, he was spotted by a Hollywood casting agent. A successful audition and two screen tests led to him being cast as Paul Atreides in Lynch's production of *Dune*.

It's perhaps hard to appreciate now, since in the event *Dune* fared so poorly, but to appear in this $50-million movie was about the biggest break any young actor could possibly have had. If it had been the box-office success that the producers had hoped for MacLachlan would have starred in sequels to the film through the decade. So in terms of his career *Blue Velvet* was a bit of a comedown from what might have been.

MacLachlan nearly lost the part of Atreides because at his audition he had a punk haircut. It undermined the look of the messiah figure he was supposed to play. But such ambiguity was welcome in *Blue Velvet*, where Jeffrey wears a gold ring in his left ear. The suggestion was of the regular guy who, however, has dared to take a walk on the wild side.

'I'm a pretty unsophisticated guy from Yakima, Washington State, who became an actor,' MacLachlan said of himself in an interview, echoing the kind of things Lynch – who spent much of his childhood in Washington – has said of himself. MacLachlan's potential as an alter ego was plain. Newspaper profiles of actor and director are striking in their similarities. In both cases interviewers always seemed to be taken aback by their apparent normality. 'MacLachlan seems to have the soul of a Boy Scout,' commented a profile in the *Daily Mail*. 'You feel he would have been perfectly cast as **James Stewart**'s son in a Western.' Lynch also was always being compared to James Stewart – and had actually been an Eagle Scout, the top kind of scout you could be in **America**.

After *Blue Velvet* MacLachlan went on to play Special Agent Dale Cooper in *Twin Peaks*, a sort of Jeffrey Beaumont grown up. He won a Golden Globe Award for the role, and to date it seems like the highpoint of his career. Nothing has really stood out since. The mainstream stardom he might have looked forward to when he won the leading role in *Dune* has continued to elude him. If that had ever been an aspiration, then the association with David Lynch was a mixed blessing.

Blue Velvet may have been a cult success, but this almost by definition meant that it was inconsequential in box-office terms – its entire US gross was a fraction of *Dune*'s production budget. *Twin Peaks* topped the ratings – briefly – but turned out to be too wilful to settle down into a profitable formula like its imitators. It lasted two seasons, while the *X-Files*, into its fifth and now a feature film too, looks as if it will never end.

Twin Peaks brought MacLachlan far more public recognition than *Blue Velvet* had ever done, but presented him with the dilemma of how to move on from a part with which he had become so strongly identified. In 1991 he played the keyboard player Ray Manzarek in the Oliver Stone movie *The Doors*. The following year he returned with some reluctance to play Special Agent Dale Cooper in the *Twin Peaks* movie *Fire Walk With Me*. Its disastrous critical reception would only have encouraged his determination to live down the character as fast as possible. In 1993 he played the villain Cliff Vandercave in the forgettable *Flintstones* movie, and he was Joseph K in an unremarkable BBC production of *The Trial*. This last seems like one of the great missed opportunities in contemporary cinema. How wonderful it would have been to have brought MacLachlan and Lynch, the **Kafka** devotee, together again on such a project.

Probably MacLachlan's worst hiccup in recent years was to appear in Paul Verhoeven's $40-million *Showgirls*, about a Las Vegas newcomer who sleeps her way to stardom. The film was condemned by most critics as soft porn and attracted an NC-17 rating – the new equivalent of the dreaded X certificate. The film bombed at the box office, and MacLachlan suffered the indignity of being nominated for a 1996 Razzie Award for Worst Actor. But one can understand why he would have wanted to work for Verhoeven, a genuinely talented director, and he deserves admiration for taking the risk in what was obviously going to be a controversial film. Most 'stars' would have played safe. His most recent appearance was in Mike Figgis's *One Night Stand*, unfortunately another disappointment at the box-office.

Asked in a recent interview if he ever got fed up with people mentioning 'damn fine coffee' to him, MacLachlan replied, 'No, not at all. It's nice to be remembered for something.'

Meadow Lane

It's rather a pretty name, conjuring up visions of a picturesque nook in the country, but it's where Frank takes his victims. Jeffrey is beaten up here.

Mike

Sandy's boyfriend, played by Ken Stovitz. He scarcely figures in the film. Early on we see him at his football practice, when he spots Sandy going off with Jeffrey. He doesn't say anything, but he is obviously upset. Then in the later stages, as Sandy and Jeffrey drive back together from a party, he chases them in his car and confronts Jeffrey outside his house. But he quickly retires into the background when the naked Dorothy emerges from the bushes.

In the script Mike is much more of a character. He makes his main appearance as a fellow guest of Jeffrey's at a dinner given by the Williamses. He is depicted as increasingly suspicious and jealous of Jeffrey. He emerges as a rather ridiculous figure, obsessed by sport and keeping fit. While everyone else drinks beer, he drinks water. He asks if anyone minds him taking his vitamins. 'The body is like a machine,' he explains. 'Everything has got to stay in perfect tune for perfect health.'

It's a mildly comic vignette, but unnecessary. The dinner party scene in which it occurs intrudes between Jeffrey spying on Frank from Dorothy's **closet** and his report to Sandy of the horrors he's seen. Its inclusion would have dissipated the mood at a critical point.

misogyny

One of the more absurd accusations levelled against David Lynch. Dorothy may be a deeply troubled woman who likes to be hit, but she is portrayed with truth and sympathy.

See **sickest film ever made?**; **therapy**; **voyeurism**.

mood

If *Blue Velvet* is a realistic film, then it is so because it shows the world not as it is or even as we perceive it to be, but rather as we *feel* it to be. 'It is in the brain that everything takes place,' wrote Oscar Wilde. 'We now know that we do not see with the eyes or hear with the ears. They are really channels for the transmission, adequate or inadequate, of sense impressions.' Wilde also wrote of 'truth in art' as 'that in which the outward is expressive of the inward'. Few roses are as red as those we see in *Blue Velvet*, few apartments so full of cavernous **darkness** as Dorothy's, but they express moods with which we are all familiar.

music

Just as *Blue Velvet* embraces several **genres**, it blends together several different types of music – the romantic score of a traditional Hollywood film, love ballads, jazz, blues and soul. The film music opening which accompanies the credits is evocative of a much earlier golden age of cinema. Its juxtaposition with the title song 'Blue Velvet' is a sharp contrast of style that warns us that things are not what they seem. In this it parallels the visual switch from the dreamy opening images to Mr Beaumont being struck down while watering his lawn. The sheer variety of the music enhances the film's feel of passing through several **periods** without belonging to any, lending it a timeless, universal quality.

Lynch heard Bobby Vinton singing 'Blue Velvet' in the early seventies and it sparked off the images which led to the movie. The song is about a man's longing for a woman he had once known. It may be one of the most overworked themes in popular music, but the song possesses a lingering, tactile quality and a sense of atmosphere which would have appealed to Lynch. More than most songs, it painted a picture.

Blue Velvet is about a man's obsession with a woman, but also it's about the power of music. Dorothy is a singer, and it's hearing her song that bewitches Frank. He's similarly overcome when he hears the Roy Orbison song 'In Dreams'. He has to switch off the cassette to keep control. Odysseus had to be tied to a mast to resist the lethal song of the Sirens, and Frank is every bit as vulnerable.

But although Frank can be deeply disturbed by music, he also uses it to communicate. He mouths the words of 'In Dreams' as a threat before beating Jeffrey up in **Meadow Lane**. He also delivers an ominous warning that Jeffrey should stay away from Dorothy – a warning couched in the words of another song ('Love Letters'). 'Don't be a good neighbor to her or I'm gonna send you a love letter, straight from my heart, fucker. You know what a love letter is? It's a bullet. Straight from my gun, fucker. Once you get a love letter from me, you're fucked for ever.'

The nature of Frank's love letters is seen in the film's finale. Jeffrey discovers the corpses of the Yellow Man and Don in Dorothy's apartment. The bloody marks of bullets – straight from Frank's gun – are prominent gashes in their foreheads. On the soundtrack Ketty Lester sings the first lines of the song that, like 'In Dreams', Frank has made his own: 'Love letters straight from your heart/Keep us so near while apart/I'm not alone in the night/When I can have all the love

you write.' The song bridges two scenes. Jeffrey hears on the Yellow
Man's radio the communications of the police surrounding Frank's
hideout, and, as the song continues, there's a switch to this scene:
a window being riddled with bullets. It's an arresting connection
between the slaughter in Dorothy's apartment and the destruction
that the **Lumberton** police visit on Frank's. There's a wanton quality
to the bullets tearing into the masonry. In an echo of Frank's taunt
to Jeffrey, 'You're like me', 'Love Letters' draws the two scenes of
violence together. It's a brilliant enlargement of meaning.

'Blue Velvet', 'In Dreams' and 'Love Letters' are the only 'found'
songs in the film. The way these once-innocent love ballads were
refashioned into messages of violence and obsession offered a musical
expression of man's **dual** nature. They became an intimate part of the
film's meaning. Remarkably, Lynch would achieve the same control
over the film score as he had over the film itself.

Before *Blue Velvet* he had found commercial cinema's approach to
film scores frustrating:

> You rarely get to sit down with the composer until late in the
> game – post-production. You meet him, you tell him what you
> want, he sees the film, comes back with the score, and there's no
> more time . . . A lot of music just gets overlaid over sequences
> and it's the composer's sole interpretation of what you've done.
> And it may or may not marry.

What he needed was a genuine **collaboration** – someone he could
interact with and who would be in tune with his overall vision for the
film. Luck provided him with **Angelo Badalamenti**. When Isabella
Rossellini was having difficulties singing the title song the producer
Fred Caruso suggested that a friend of his – Badalamenti – coach her.
Lynch was sceptical, but in the end was delighted with the result.
Then Lynch had wanted to use This Mortal Coil's recording of Tim

Buckley's 'Song to a Siren' for the love scene between Jeffrey and
Sandy, but the permissions fee was too expensive. So Caruso suggested
that, instead, Lynch should write his own lyrics and get Badalamenti
to do the music. Once more Lynch was sceptical: 'A song to take
the place of *this* song, out of millions of songs, this *one* song that I
have to have, Fred? And you're telling me to write *lyrics* and give
them to Angelo, and this is going to solve my problems!' But once
more he gave it a go. Badalamenti got a friend of his, Julee Cruise,
to sing 'Mysteries of Love' and Lynch was so pleased that he asked
Badalamenti to do the music for the whole film.

Blue Velvet would mark the beginning of a close musical collaboration that extended beyond films, as they began to produce albums
together. It was one more example of Lynch's intuitive approach.
Although not musically trained, he could hear music perfectly and
knew exactly when something was what he wanted.

Badalamenti has described their working method: 'David does not
compose music himself. He just tells me, "Take me to the abstract
world." It could be dark, eccentric, bitter, sweet or tragically beautiful, and I have to translate his words into music.' Badalamenti has
called Lynch – in terms of music – his 'second wife', and it seems
appropriate that their first full collaboration should have been on the
song 'Mysteries of Love'. If Lynch was living with some degree of
musical confusion before, all became clear with the arrival of Angelo
Badalamenti.

Badalamenti made it possible for him to make the score as integral
a part of the meaning of the film as the songs. One of the satisfactions
of *Blue Velvet* is to see this crucial element in the cinema, usually so
disjointed, contributing to an organic whole. Lynch had managed to
escape the tyranny of traditional film music whereby it is applied – as
Michael Powell once memorably put it – to the dialogue and sound
effects 'like the rich glazing on a ham'.

Badalamenti's music for *Blue Velvet*, it seems to me, is one of the great film scores of modern times. It not so much complements the images as seems to grow out of them. And it stands so well by itself. Listening to the soundtrack album, you don't have that sense of divorce you normally have when listening to a movie soundtrack. The music contains within it the film's dark essence. To listen to the album separately, with the afterglow of the images in your mind, even enriches your appreciation.

When Sandy and Jeffrey sit in the **darkness** outside the church, this scene of despair and confusion is accompanied by the strains of organ music. In the film you only get a small part of a piece, which runs nearly five minutes on the album. Listening to the CD, you feel the full force of what is necessarily in the film – where the music is just one element – a more subliminal impression. At first I was surprised to learn from the album notes that I was listening to an instrumental version of 'Mysteries of Love'. Listening to it again, I realised that indeed it was, but the melody was missing. The rich chords, without the register of the tune, leave you feeling rather queasy. It's like being lost at sea, which of course is how Sandy and Jeffrey are feeling. It's music without any **robins**. The piece is heard again when Sandy and Jeffrey kiss at a party and realise that they are in love. But this time the voice of Julee Cruise supplies the missing melody. It is the answer to the earlier puzzle, the musical fulfilment of Sandy's dream.

'Mysteries of Love', the song that only came about because Lynch couldn't afford the permissions fee for the song he actually wanted to use – Tim Buckley's 'Song for a Siren' – grew in importance to become the key song of the entire film. It surges on to the soundtrack at several points. Like some musical guardian angel, it's a fortifying presence. It's there in the moments of despair – so we hear it when a deeply despondent Jeffrey tells Sandy about Frank, hear it too as Sandy tries to come to terms with the fact that Jeffrey has betrayed her. And it's there in the moments of clarity and happiness. After Frank has been killed, as if some wicked spell has finally been lifted, it carries us through to the very end of the film, from Sandy and Jeffrey embracing outside **Deep River Apartments**, to the appearance of the robin, and then to Dorothy reunited with her son. Only then does it yield to a note of sadness as Dorothy is heard in voice-over singing a final poignant line from the title song: 'And I still can see blue velvet through my tears. . . .'

N

Nance, Jack (1943–1996)

He was Henry in *Eraserhead*, and worked on all Lynch's full-length films except for *The Elephant Man*. In *Blue Velvet* he played a small but memorable role as one of Frank's henchmen, Paul – although 'playing a role' seems hardly the right way to put it.

Of all Lynch's actors, the line between the characters he played and his own life seemed the narrowest. Ten years after *Blue Velvet* he got into a fight with two men outside a doughnut shop in Pasadena, where he lived, and was hit on the head. Or at least this was the story he told two friends before one of them found him dead in his apartment the next day. But the police were never too sure what had really happened. One of the officers on the case thought it more likely that he had just got drunk and banged his head.

Born in Dallas in 1943, he discovered acting while at North Texas State University. He gave up a degree in journalism in order to devote himself to it, and studied at the Dallas Theatre Center. He moved on to California, where he worked briefly at the Pasadena Playhouse and then for the Circus Theatre Company in San Francisco. The high point of his stage career was appearing in the title role of a hit play about the **American** patriot Tom Paine. When it went on tour and came to Los Angeles he was offered a guest spot on *Hawaii Five-O* but, in a decision typical of his unworldliness, turned it down because he didn't want to leave the production.

By the early seventies Nance had moved to Los Angeles, but the film offers had dried up and he was living on welfare. A friend introduced him to David Lynch, who was casting for *Eraserhead*. Lynch recalled the occasion as 'a fairly strange, uneasy meeting'. Nance seemed bored. But then on his way back to his car he admired the wooden roof-rack of Lynch's old Volkswagen and his enthusiasm sudenly became apparent.

Lynch described Nance as 'a zero-motivated actor, content to stay at home, not even watching television, just sitting in his chair wearing his little slippers'. It made him perfect for Henry in *Eraserhead*, but meant that his film roles would be few. 'He's a strange guy and doesn't go out looking for work,' Lynch commented. 'If you wanted him for a film, you'd have to go get him and dust him off.' That's what happened on *Blue Velvet*. After working for Lynch on **Dune** Nance, sick of LA, drifted back to his hometown, Dallas, from where Lynch had to fetch him. 'I always say,' commented Nance in an interview, 'I hope David never discovers that he can make a picture without me because I might never work again.'

Of Paul, his character in *Blue Velvet*, he commented he 'was a pretty sick character but that might be because I was a pretty sick character at the time, too'. Nance, a chronic alcoholic, was drinking heavily and towards the end of shooting asked Dennis Hopper to help him give up. Hopper, who had fought his own battle against addiction, put Nance in touch with a rehabilitation clinic in Los Angeles.

Sober for the first time in years, he appeared in *Barfly*, in Hopper's *Colors* and *The Hot Spot*, and then as Pete Martell in Lynch's *Twin Peaks*. Things seemed to be going well, but the clouds were soon to return. In late 1991 his second wife – an addict whom he had met in the rehabilitation unit – hanged herself. Two years later Nance started drinking again.

In Ben's place Paul's sidekick Raymond releases and retracts a switchblade, joking, 'Here today, gone tomorrow!' Paul replies, 'You don't scare me,' but it turned out to be prophetic.

neighbours

Lumberton is a small town. Jeffrey and Sandy went to the same school, and their parents know one another. Jeffrey finds the severed **ear** in a field behind where he lives, and it's just a short walk from Sandy's comfortable house to the sinister **Deep River Apartments**. Sandy finds it weird that a woman who is implicated in a murder inquiry should live so close, but as the mystery unfolds she learns how goodness and evil exist side by side like neighbours.

When Frank bumps into Jeffrey at Deep River Apartments, Dorothy explains that he's 'from the neighbourhood', and henceforward Frank mockingly calls him 'Neighbour'. The word becomes an index of the bond between them.

Norris, Patricia

She began in films as a clerk in the Warner Brothers wardrobe department. She received her first credit as a costume designer for *The Good Guys and the Bad Guys* in 1969. Since then, a distinguished career has been notable for an **Oscar** jinx, whereby she has been nominated five times but not won once: *Days of Heaven*, *The Elephant Man*, *Victor/Victoria*, *2010* and *Sunset*. She deserved to win something for *Blue Velvet*. For the first time, she was not only **costume** designer but art director too. She was able to create a total look in keeping with the overall meaning and atmosphere of the film. Cinematographer **Frederick Elmes** credited her use of vivid **colour** for the painterly look of the film. 'Patty created the world that David wanted to see and yet brought something more to it. Even though it's basically a location film – there are only a couple of sets – she managed to get in there and control what was in front of the camera in a really wonderful way that I think helped the style along.'

She first worked with Lynch on *The Elephant Man* and has been a regular **collaborator** ever since. She is yet one more example of the team spirit at the heart of Lynch's film-making. 'I collaborate with Patty the same way as with everybody else and it's a process of getting everybody tuned in to the same thing,' he has said. 'She knows by now the things I like, and we talk a lot, and look at photos or drawings, or . . . whatever it takes to get the idea, and the next thing I know it's there.'

When Jeffrey visits **Deep River Apartments** there's a sense of the building being alive. There are the creaks and groans of its internal workings, but also a decor in sympathy with its forlorn tenant Dorothy Vallens. It's as if all the other inhabitants have long since fled, and she's marooned there, the bare, bruised walls projecting her despair. 'All rooms come out of people,' Norris has commented, 'and if you understand who the characters are, you understand how they live. Most decorating conveys what's not written, and gives you a sense of the people.' So in Ben's place the wallpaper partially covers over the cracks but peels away from the damp in the walls, just as Ben's peacock manners and powdered face offer no more than a thin veneer with which to hide his rotten heart.

Norris's production design closely complemented her costumes. In *Blue Velvet* she achieved a kind of '**mood**-wear' – an impressionist rather than a naturalistic rendering in fabric that expressed the characters' changing emotions with the same subtlety and regard for Lynch's overall conception as the lighting, the **sound** design or the **musical** score.

Other films include *The Candidate, The Missouri Breaks, Silent Movie, Capricorn One, Scarface, Black Widow, Wild at Heart, Twin Peaks: Fire Walk With Me, Lost Highway* and *The End of Violence*. She won an Emmy – an award at last – for her costume design on the *Twin Peaks* TV series.

O

Oscars

The only surprise is that *Blue Velvet* was put up for any. One would have thought it far too offbeat and original, but it was for one. At the 1986 Academy Awards David Lynch couldn't escape being nominated for Best Director (as he had been for ***The Elephant Man*** in 1980), an award which in the event went to Oliver Stone for the suitably conventional *Platoon*.

P

Pabst Blue Ribbon

I was curious to try it. I looked in Asda, Tesco and Sainsbury's. They stocked Jeffrey's beer, Heineken, Detective Williams's beer, Budweiser, but not Frank's favourite beer, Pabst Blue Ribbon. It seemed like a missed opportunity. With a picture of Frank on the side of the can it would sell really well. There's even the perfect advertisement for it in the film. 'What kinda beer do you drink?' Frank asks Jeffrey, as they enter Ben's place. 'Heineken,' he replies. 'Fuck that shit!' shouts Frank. 'Pabst Blue Ribbon!'

But drinking beer is just one way in which Frank gets his kicks: there are the **drugs** he takes, the people he beats up and the songs he listens to. At Ben's we see him do all four in one night.

Blue Velvet, which is called after Frank's fetish, is about the power of spells, the danger of losing your mind to them. It's in the nature of a spell that there should be no explanation for its hold; it is beyond reason. The blue velvet, which could as easily be anything else, becomes a symbol for the sheer infinity of spells which can hold us in thrall.

painting

Lynch's first love was painting, and to appreciate his films it helps to realise that he never stopped being a painter. When he first began to use film at art school it was less a switch into a different medium than a case of an artist seeking to extend his range. Lynch's account of how he first became interested in film conveys the organic nature of the process. An almost-black painting of his hung in a large room in the Pennsylvania Academy of Fine Art, and in the middle there was a figure. 'I'm looking at this figure in the painting, and I hear a little wind, and see a little movement. And I had a wish that the painting would really be able to move, you know, some little bit. And that was it.'

Attuned to paradox and contradiction, it is characteristic that Lynch should operate on the point of tension between two media. The titles of many of his paintings – like *Suddenly my House Became a Tree of Sores* or *Shadow of a Twisted Hand Across My House* – suggest an urge for movement and narrative, just as his films suggest a painter's regard for composition and texture.

When Lynch talks about the inspiration for his paintings, he could as easily be talking about his films. 'A lot of my paintings come from memories of Boise, Idaho, and Spokane, . . . I like to think about a neighbourhood like a fence, like a ditch, and somebody digging a hole, and then a girl in this house, and a tree, and what's happening in that tree – a little local place that I can get into.'

Blue Velvet was a similar coalescence of memories and ideas. Listening to the Bobby Vinton song 'Blue Velvet' made him think about things: 'And the first things I thought about were lawns – lawns and the neighbourhood.' The look was inspired by his childhood in Spokane, Washington. It turned out to be a movie, but the thought process could as easily have led to a painting. So many of the concerns of *Blue Velvet* are to be found in the Lynch paintings. In the painting *I See Myself*, for example, two skeletal figures face each other on either side of a rough diagonal line – one light, one so dark that it almost fades into the blackness of the background. The themes of this picture – the darkness, the idea of looking, the dual nature of personality, the general atmosphere of anxiety – are all familiar from Lynch's movies. 'The paintings have a fearful mood, but there's humour in them too. But ultimately, I guess the central idea is, you know, life in darkness and confusion.'

See **Bacon, Francis**; **Hopper, Edward**; **influences**.

paradise lost

The **American** paradise of **Lumberton**'s white-picket fences and tree-lined avenues where Sandy and Jeffrey live belongs to an idealised **fifties**. The world of **drugs** which Frank inhabits belongs to the venal **eighties**. In the collision of these two worlds Lynch paints a portrait of a paradise already containing the seeds of its own destruction.

I'm not sure that Lumberton could ever exist in reality. It embraces too much difference. It seems to me more a place of the mind, fusing together Lynch's small-town childhood and the big cities he would live in when he was grown-up. It reminds me of those old allegorical paintings, where all the stages in the spiritual progress of man – from his loss of innocence to his redemption – are represented in a single landscape. In this modern version of the Garden of Eden myth, small-town America is the paradise; Jeffrey is Adam; Sandy is Eve handing him the apple; and Dorothy, the temptation to which he succumbs.

Paul

One of Frank's henchmen, a cameo part memorably played by Jack Nance.

★   ★   ★

people like Frank

Every Saturday morning when we do our shopping we run into the Dog Man. He's a frightening spectacle we can't help staring at. There's something menacing about the way he strides up the supermarket aisles. The permanent scowl on his face suggests that his athletic energy would more naturally express itself in violence. The contents of his shopping trolley add to the impression of a man disturbingly off-kilter. Just heaps of dog food and beer. Nothing else. He's like a fierce dog himself, a lean Rottweiler. One Saturday we shared the lift to the car park with him. He thumped the button as if he was trying to break it. My eyes briefly connected with his. 'DON'T FUCKING LOOK AT ME!' his answering glare seemed to shout. I quickly looked down at my shoes. We unloaded our shopping and got in the car. On our way back home, the Dog Man drove up fast behind us and, almost bumper to bumper, hooted several times. Frightened, we pulled over to the side of the road and he sped off.

Every time I see him I think of Jeffrey's despairing cry, 'Why are there people like Frank? Why is there so much trouble in this world?'

Blue Velvet may contain the exaggeration of art, but its starting-point is reality. The people like Frank are out there, and we get glimpses of them occasionally.

period

'The fashions in cars, clothes and music are deliberately confused so that we cannot tell precisely when it is taking place,' wrote the film critic Philip French. 'A roadside hoarding, for instance, reading "Welcome to **Lumberton**", bears the face of a woman out of a 1950s *Life* magazine, but the middle-class hero has a gold ring in his left ear.' I don't think it's that Lynch consciously sets out to confuse us. I think it's more that he borrows period details with their varying associations and, however anachronistic they may appear outwardly, uses them to build up a **mood**.

In creating the serene and ordered façade of his small town he returns to the **fifties** because that was the decade in which he had felt most secure and in which **America** appeared most confident and at ease with itself. But these images are deployed in such a way as to give a sense that they are only a façade and to imply the hidden world behind. The roadside hoarding, for example, is just a two-dimensional flat board, and it's juxtaposed with the sequence in which, following Mr Beaumont's collapse, the camera penetrates the surface of his lawn to reveal the bugs scrambling in the depths. The message is plain: these images of innocence are not what they seem.

They gain an emotive strength because we bring to them our contemporary awareness. The only picture Sandy has on her bedroom wall is one of Montgomery Clift. The association of her with this fifties star who had a hidden side says a lot about the sort of person she is. The same picture on a teenage girl's bedroom wall in the fifties would have had a completely different set of connotations.

Peyton Place

This hit **fifties** film was a spiritual ancestor of *Blue Velvet*. It too explored the **dark** side of a small **American** town and – just as *Blue Velvet* led to *Twin Peaks* – spawned a hugely successful soap opera.

See **Lange, Hope**.

★   ★   ★

Philadelphia

'As W. C. Fields said, I'd rather be here than Philadelphia,' comments Kyle MacLachlan as he drives into Twin Peaks for the first time. Like **Deep River Apartments**, Philadelphia is a place of ambivalence – a place of great danger, but where there is much to learn. Lynch has described the city as the biggest influence in his life. It was the place where he 'woke up'. When he was 19 he went to art school there, but the most important lessons were to be learnt in the streets of the city itself. He lived in a poor part of town with his young wife and **child**. Their house was burgled several times, their windows shot out and a car stolen. In Philadelphia he discovered fear but, as significantly, just how consuming a **mood** can be. 'All that protected us from the outside were these bricks. But the bricks might as well have been paper. The feeling was so close to extreme danger, and the fear was so intense.'

But he relished the atmosphere of 'factories, smoke, railroads, diners, the strangest characters and the darkest nights'. He found the city 'frightening, but more than that, *thrilling*'. The impact would have been all the greater for the tranquillity of his upbringing in small-town **America**. In *Blue Velvet* he brought these two worlds together to suggest that evil – or its opposite – can emerge out of anywhere. It is the sort of irony Lynch would probably appreciate that 'Philadephia', one of the most violent cities in America, should mean 'the city of brotherly love'.

plot

The narrative of *Blue Velvet* is untidy. The reasons why characters do things are often imprecise. It's easy to pick holes in the plot.

Jeffrey has been told by Sandy that a woman called Dorothy Vallens is somehow mixed up in the case of the severed **ear**, but it seems odd that he should then want to sneak into her apartment when he has never seen her before and when, as Sandy makes clear, she has already been under police surveillance for two months. If it's information about the case he wants, he would do better to persuade Sandy to do some more eavesdropping on her father's conversations.

Jeffrey's plan is that he will gain entry to Dorothy's apartment by disguising himself as a pest-control man. Sandy, disguised as a Jehovah's witness, will then knock on Dorothy's door, and the few seconds' distraction will give him a chance to open a window, through which he will be able to crawl later. Yet the fact that the apartment is on the seventh floor makes this plan seem pretty useless.

Their visit to **the Slow Club** to watch Dorothy sing on the night that Jeffrey sneaks into Dorothy's apartment seems astonishingly reckless. Rather than waste precious time watching her show, it would have made more sense to wait for her to leave her apartment and then sneak in.

At the end of the film it is not explained why Jeffrey should want to return to Dorothy's apartment as the police move in on Frank's **gang**. There is nothing he could have expected to find there; it just seems total chance that he comes upon the corpse of the Yellow Man and Dorothy's husband, Don. Nor is it clear why Frank should return to the apartment, from which he can only have recently left after killing the Yellow Man and Dorothy's husband. How does he know that Jeffrey will be there? The showdown does not develop logically out of the narrative.

Before setting off to **Deep River Apartments** Jeffrey rings Sandy and tells her to get her father to go there. When Sandy rings the police she's told that they don't know Detective Williams's whereabouts, yet shortly afterwards the detective's seen directing an operation that must involve practically the whole of the **Lumberton** police force.

If Lynch had not enjoyed the privilege of the final cut, if the film had been a *studio* film instead of a personal film, the script would doubtless have been given a major overhaul. A team of writers would have ironed out the inconsistencies, made sure that every occurrence had a crystal-clear explanation and honed characters of easily comprehensible motivation. In short, they would have made a completely different film. For the power of *Blue Velvet* lies in its embrace of **mood** over narrative logic, in its recognition that the reasons why people do things are often mysterious, that the world has none of the certainty that Hollywood craves.

With its hoodlums and car chases, *Blue Velvet* has many of the trappings of a Hollywood movie but a different operating system. It has the logic of a dream, where you find yourself in situations without knowing how you got into them, where events and settings reflect an inner rather than an outer reality. It is less a linear narrative than a coalescence of concerns. And in this landscape of the mind the normal rules of time and place are secondary.

Jeffrey sees Frank at the end because he's *got* to see Frank, Frank is on his mind. It's as if some mental energy calls their showdown into being. If their meeting strains narrative plausibility, this makes its emotional necessity all the stronger. Similarly, when Sandy runs frantically through the streets to be with Jeffrey nothing in the narrative has alerted her to the trouble he is in, but this makes the sense of her intuitive knowledge all the more powerful.

A comparison of the script of *Blue Velvet* with the finished film reveals someone pursuing an opposite path to that of the conventional Hollywood scriptwriter. Right from the beginning there were loose ends that the script editors would have tidied up. As Mr Beaumont has his stroke and collapses to the ground a little boy licking a lollipop toddles on to the scene. There is no explanation of who he is. The film just switches, via the bugs in the Beaumonts' lawn, to Jeffrey visiting his father in hospital. In the script this little boy had both a name, Gregg, and a narrative purpose – he is the means by which

Mr Beaumont is found. As his mother summons him home, she spots the stricken figure. Once Lynch had decided not to show Mr Beaumont being discovered, there was no longer any narrative reason for the boy to remain – the script editors would have taken him out completely – but his unexplained presence in the film lends an extra quality to the scene: there's a neighbourhood feel – in neighbourhoods little boys often are just around without there having to be a reason – and also a pathos in the contrast between the young boy at the start of his life and a man near the end of his. Pruned of the narrative strings, an incident which would otherwise have been a flat A-to-B moment takes on depth and richness.

Sandy's magical first appearance after Jeffrey visits her father was another example of Lynch cutting through narrative banality. In the script Jeffrey arrives at the Williamses to find that Detective Williams hasn't got back home yet. Mrs Williams invites him to have a cup of coffee and a slice of cake while he waits for him to return. Sandy and her boyfriend Mike come into the kitchen and Mrs Willams introduces Jeffrey to them. 'Mike's gotta go,' Sandy says and escorts him outside. Detective Williams comes home and Jeffrey has his chat with him. He then meets Sandy again as he leaves. In the film the earlier scene in which Sandy is seen in the house with Mike is cut. So when Jeffrey meets her outside, it is for the first time. As there's no explanation of what she's doing outside, she becomes a wonderful vision of purity emanating out of the darkness rather than a teenager who's just said goodbye to her boyfriend.

A story can be a wonderful thing – it's the fount of Hollywood's continuing power – but it also brings with it a tyranny. As it drives forward, you must keep your eyes on the road ahead, anticipate what is round the corner rather than linger on the scenery through which you have just passed. Lynch's adjustments to his script toned down the engine of narrative and freed his audience to imagine.

124 MOVIE GUIDE

Pointer, Priscilla (b. 1924)

She trained at the Tamara Daykarhanova School for the Stage. She married the theatre director Jules Irving in 1947. Irving co-founded the San Francisco Actors' Workshop in 1952, and then from 1965 ran the prestigious Lincoln Center Repertory Theater in New York. A regular performer for both theatre companies, Pointer didn't embark on a TV and film career until the seventies. By the time of *Blue Velvet* she had become well practised at playing mothers. In Brian De Palma's *Carrie* she was the mother of Carrie's best friend Sue Snell (played by her real-life daughter Amy Irving), and in the early eighties she made regular appearances in the soap operas *Dallas* and *Knots Landing* as Rebecca Blake Barnes, the mother of Pamela Ewing. She was also – briefly – Steven Spielberg's mother-in-law.

Other films include *Nickleodeon*, *Looking for Mr Goodbar*, *Gray Lady Down*, *The Onion Field*, *Mommie Dearest*, *The Falcon and the Snowman*, *Rumpelstiltskin* and *Disturbed*. She won a Critics' Circle Award nomination for her performance in the TV film *Eleanor and Franklin*.

providence

Blue Velvet was shot mostly in and around Wilmington, North Carolina, where De Laurentiis's Entertainment Group had just built a new studio. If De Laurentiis's move dictated the choice of town, it was just a small example of Lynch making the most of circumstances. Providence was a crucial ingredient at every stage in the film's making.

Lynch received the finishing touches of *Blue Velvet* in a dream:

> The dream gave me the police radio; the dream gave me Frank's disguise; the dream gave me the gun in the Yellow Man's jacket; the dream gave me the scene where Jeffrey was

Sandy's bedroom wall there's a poster of Montgomery Clift – the kind of man with a hidden side that she seems to be attracted to. (BFI)

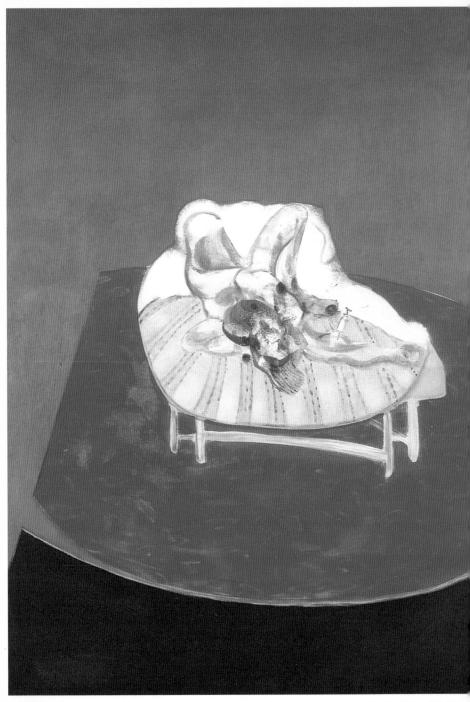

Lying Figure with Hypodermic Syringe, 1963. (©The Estate of Francis Bacon/ARS, NY and DACS, London 1998)

David Lynch meets Francis Bacon: Dorothy alone in her apartment all disguise removed now. (BFI)

Scottie (James Stewart) seeing double in *Vertigo*. (BFI)

Jeffrey torn between sacred and profane love in *Blue Velvet*. (BFI)

While Jeffrey steps into a closet to do his spying, in *Rear Window* his near namesake L.B. Jefferies (James Stewart) takes advantage of a telephoto lens. Behind him stands his girlfriend Lisa (Grace Kelly). Like Sandy – wearing a splendid floral dress – Lisa comes to the rescue of her man in the end. (Corbis/Everett)

Love and Death: still wearing her debutante's dress, Sandy arrives at Deep River Apartments a split second after Jeffrey has blown Frank's brains out. (BFI)

Twin Peaks was a reworking of *Blue Velvet*'s dualist themes for primetime TV. Whether the twin peaks and forked waterfall of the opening credits, or the paired characters, or the Double R diner, or even Audrey's two-tone shoes, the number 2 prevailed. (Corbis/Everett)

Sandy (Olivia Newton-John), the innocent high-school girl in *Grease*: an earlier exercise in Fifties retro. (BFI)

in the back of Dorothy's apartment, sending the wrong message, knowing Frank would hear it. I don't know how it happened, but I just had to plug and change a few things to bring it all together.

To explain the way he works David Lynch has often used the analogy of fishing: 'If you're quiet and sitting there and you have the right bait you're going to catch a fish eventually. Ideas are sort of like that. You never know when they are going to hit you.' The impression he gives is of someone who does not make things up but is responding to something 'out there'. *Blue Velvet* had its own independent life, in which these unforeseen ideas produced something much better than Lynch could have consciously worked out, although whatever chance presented he would then rigorously fashion into an appropriate pattern. This responsiveness led to several important sequences which were not in the original script being added in the course of production.

On the way to Wilmington from New York Lynch heard the Roy Orbison song 'Crying' on a taxi cab's radio. Instantly he wanted to use it in the film. But back in Wilmington he listened to a record of Orbison's greatest hits and forgot all about 'Crying' when he heard 'In Dreams'. The song 'explained to me so much of what the film was all about'.

Lynch imagined a scene in which Dennis Hopper, as Frank, would sing 'In Dreams' in Ben's place. Unknown to him, Hopper and Dean Stockwell (Ben) worked together on their own version of the scene. In rehearsal they both began to sing the song. Then Hopper stopped singing and looked at Stockwell with an expression of being moved as Stockwell continued to sing: 'There was the scene in front of me. It was so perfect.' Stockwell provided another perfect touch by using the wrong prop to sing the song. Lynch had intended that he would use a small candle-style table lamp as a microphone, but Stockwell picked up a studio work light instead: 'He turned it and flipped the long cord like a microphone cord and obviously it couldn't have been more perfect. The strange thing is no one on the crew put that work light there. No one knew where it came from. Who can say how it happens?'

It's in talking about the source of his creative ideas that David Lynch can seem most like Frank. He gives an impression, like Frank, of being in thrall to a force greater than himself. 'In Dreams', a song discovered by accident – or sent by providence – was a special song for both of them. 'In dreams I walk with you/In dreams I talk with you' – while Frank mouths these words as a threat to Jeffrey that he can never escape him, in Lynch's case they sum up a process of inspiration: 'A film exists somewhere before you do it. It's sitting in some abstract world, complete, and you're just listening to it talk to you, telling you the way it's supposed to be.' The chief difference is that Lynch is able to harness the force controlling him in a positive way. 'A lot more happens when you open yourself up to the work and let yourself act and react to it. Every work "talks" to you, and if you listen to it, it will take you places you never dreamed of. It's this inter-action that makes the work richer.'

pussy heaven

Ben's place is informally known as this by Frank's **gang**. By the entrance there hangs a picture of a half-naked woman reclining on a bed. It makes the business of the place clear. When Frank and the boys arrive, it has the deserted feel of a Second World War airbase during a raid. The girls are out working.

R

Raymond

One of Frank's henchmen. He's played by Brad Dourif, who first
came to prominence as Billy Bibbit, the stuttering mental patient
who commits suicide in *One Flew Over the Cuckoo's Nest*. With a
hank of hair flopping down over one eye, he seems a bit of a misfit
– less a hoodlum than someone slow-witted and easily led astray.
Probably he was friendless and picked on at school. As Billy Bibbit
found a protector in Randle Patrick McMurphy, Raymond finds one
in Frank, but a dangerous and unpredictable one. When he takes too
long over pouring the beers at Ben's place, Frank jumps on him:
'Pour the fuckin' beer!' But frightened and vulnerable, Raymond's
prepared to risk Frank's tantrums for the camaraderie of the **gang**.

Rear Window

Made in 1954, Hitchcock's *Rear Window* is perhaps the daddy of
peeping-Tom films. Lynch has spoken of his admiration for it, and
its influence on *Blue Velvet* seems considerable.

James Stewart plays a photographer confined to his apartment
with a broken leg. He whiles away his time by looking through his
neighbours' windows. In the evenings he's visited by his girlfriend
Lisa, played by Grace Kelly. In the whole course of the film he never
leaves his apartment. We get to know it as well as Dorothy's. 'You
know in the old days they used to put your eyes out with a red
hot poker,' warns his nurse when she catches him spying on his

neighbours. 'We've become a race of peeping Toms. What people ought to do is get outside their houses and look in for a change.'

Rear Window works on two levels, concerned as much with what Stewart learns about himself as the evidence he uncovers that one of his neighbours is a murderer. Stewart loves Grace Kelly but hesitates to take the plunge and marry her. What he sees through his neighbours' windows offers different perspectives on human relationships. There's Miss Lonely Hearts, who entertains an imaginary lover but cannot cope when she has a real one. There's a childless couple, who pour all their love into their dog. There's Miss Torso, the ballet dancer, always surrounded by gentlemen admirers and 'juggling wolves', as Grace Kelly puts it. And, finally, there's the husband who will murder his bedridden wife. None of these dramas encourages a positive attitude to domestic commitment, but Grace Kelly will prove her resourcefulness and – fulfilling the nurse's words about looking in for a change – demonstrate to Stewart that it is up to them to make their own happiness in their own way.

The James Stewart character is called L. B. Jefferies and is referred to throughout as 'Jeff'. Whether or not Lynch made a conscious borrowing, it's appropriate that Jeffrey in *Blue Velvet* should have the same name; the **voyeurism** of both the characters causes them to embark upon a rite of passage that leaves them better equipped to progress in the adult world. By the end of *Rear Window* James Stewart is finally able to commit himself to Grace Kelly, as at the end of *Blue Velvet* Jeffrey does to Sandy.

The blonde Lisa seems as much a model for Sandy as L. B. Jeffries is for Jeffrey Beaumont. Lisa and Sandy share a 'feminine intuition' and both overcome their cautious natures to risk extreme danger – Lisa sneaking into the murderer's apartment to find the vital evidence Jeff is looking for; Sandy coming to Jeffrey's aid in **Deep River Apartments**. 'You're not up on your private eye literature,' says Lisa to Jeff. 'When they're in trouble it's always their girl Friday who gets them out of it.' There's even a visual resemblance. Both girls, as they prove themselves in the final scenes, wear floral-patterned dresses.

When Jeff first begins to suspect that something is amiss he consults Lieutenant Tom Doyle. The lieutenant's an old friend of Jeff's just as in *Blue Velvet* Detective Williams knows Jeffrey's father. It's a measure of the difference between **the fifties** and **the eighties** that Lynch's detective is much more ready to suspect the worst. In contrast, Doyle chides Jeff for his nosiness. 'That's a secret private world you're looking into out there. People do a lot of things in private that they couldn't possibly explain in public.'

He means peculiar but fundamentally innocuous things. *Blue Velvet* pushes the theme of a private world to its logical limits, but *Rear Window* hesitates to dig too deep beneath a conventional morality. Stewart may have a voyeuristic streak and his neighbours may reveal themselves in a less than flattering light, but they remain far apart from the dark world of the wife murder. He is somehow beyond the pale. No sympathy is shown to him, although his situation is one of considerable pathos – a man driven to murder by the demands of an invalid wife. Finally, Hitchcock cared too much for what his audience would tolerate to portray him other than as a stereotypical villain. In contrast, Lynch not only sought to understand the behaviour of a murderous gangster, but also dared to suggest that the hero might share some of his dark instincts.

Five years after *Rear Window* a film was made about a voyeur who kills people. It paid the price for treating its subject with compassion. 'The only really satisfactory way of disposing of *Peeping Tom* would be to shovel it up and flush it swiftly down the nearest sewer. Even then the stench would remain,' wrote one critic in a review that reflected the general response.

Blue Velvet belongs to the *Peeping Tom* tradition. It may not actively enlist sympathy for Frank, who has none of Mark Lewis's gentleness, but it suggests that there is something essentially human about the impulses that drive him. His evil is not an alien aberration but a reflection of what mankind is capable of.

robins

They are the symbols of love that Sandy tells Jeffrey about in her dream. The world will be dark until the robins come. One robin does arrive at the end of the film, but just as one swallow doesn't make a summer, one doubts that this lone presence will be enough. Its value as a harbinger of happier times is further undermined by the fact that it's plainly mechanical and has a bug in its beak, presumably picked out from the monsters rampaging underneath **Mr Beaumont**'s lawn.

When **David Lynch** was growing up in Boise, Idaho, he killed a robin by throwing a clod of earth at it, and then set fire to it.

Rockwell, Norman (1894–1978)

Norman Rockwell meets Hieronymous Bosch.

This is one of the most often quoted descriptions of *Blue Velvet*, which David Lynch attributed to one of the **sound** mixers on the film. Somewhere in Stockbridge, Massachusetts, the small **American** town where he ended his days, I imagine Rockwell quietly spinning in his grave at the association. 'He did not seek out the ugly or the sordid,' wrote the curator of the Norman Rockwell Museum in the preface to a book I bought of his pictures, 'but chose to accentuate the positive in the American character.'

Rockwell was born in 1894 in New York City, where he lived for the first nine years of his life. But his family spent their summers on a farm in upstate New York, and Rockwell came to have a life-long devotion to the countryside. 'I guess I have a bad case of the American nostalgia for the clean, simple country life as opposed to the complicated world of the city.'

David Lynch enjoyed an idyllic childhood in the country, but used to visit his grandparents in New York City. 'And it scared the hell out of me . . . I had a taste of horror every time I went to New York.'

I can imagine the two in passing trains during the school holidays: Rockwell, the city kid happy to be leaving the big city behind; Lynch, the country boy filled with anxiety to be approaching it. But what if their early lives were switched over, so that Rockwell's first memory was of the country, and Lynch's the unease of the big city? Would Lynch now be making reassuring movies for Disney? And would Rockwell be remembered for those disturbing **paintings** that reveal America's dark side?

They share the same road, even if they took it in opposite directions. In 1912 Rockwell began as an illustrator for the Boy Scouts' magazine *Boy's Life*. He was for a few years the magazine's art director and his association with the Scouts was lifelong. Every year from 1925 to 1976 a Rockwell illustration appeared on the cover of the Boy Scout calendar. In one of those years, 1960, the young David Lynch was an Eagle Scout – the top kind of scout you can be. Perhaps he had a Rockwell calendar on his bedroom wall.

Very little is required for their visions of America to slide into each other. A contemporary cast of mind easily transforms Rockwell's idyll, so that collected together his pictures seem counterproductive of their original purpose. The cumulative effect is to emphasise their airbrushed nature. As you leaf through one glowing depiction of the American dream after another, they start to become rather sinister even. They have no texture, they could almost be photographs and their very flatness makes you think of a façade, a hiding of the truth.

There's a picture called *The Runaway*. A jovial policeman and a little boy sit next to each other on shiny metallic stools at the counter in a diner. 'Little boys and their red bandana satchels will forever be tempted to wander down the road apiece looking for new friends and adventures,' reads the caption. We're meant to think the policeman's saying something like, 'We'd better be taking you home to your folks.' Forty years after the picture was painted, it's too easy to imagine an alternative interpretation. A corrupt cop like **the Yellow Man** running a paedophile racket, maybe – the 'Special Today' not necessarily the meatballs.

The opening sequence of *Blue Velvet* – with its cheery guardians of civil order, the fireman and the crossing attendant – has the same quality. It's too one-sided, too good to be true. It seems to call into being the **darkness** that follows as a necessary counterbalance.

Rossellini, Isabella (b. 1952)

When David Lynch was casting parts for *Blue Velvet*, one evening in a New York restaurant a friend introduced him to Isabella Rossellini. 'You could be Ingrid Bergman's daughter,' he said, struck by her beauty.

'You idiot,' said his friend, 'she *is* Ingrid Bergman's daughter.'

Lynch was, of course, hardly the first person to comment upon the resemblance. Isabella Rossellini had spent most of her life coping with such remarks. And if living up to her mother was difficult enough, it can't have helped that her father happened to be the great Italian film director Roberto Rossellini. The spiritual presence of her parents permeates the account she gives of herself in her recent memoir, *Some of Me*. Deeply conscious of their influence, she draws on their memory to orientate herself. Her own life seems like a reconciliation of her parents' two contrasting worlds, embracing both the artist's commitment of her father, and the glamorous, materialist world of her mother, the Hollywood star.

She was born one of twins in Rome. In her early twenties she began to work as a journalist because it 'seemed serious', but this career took a frivolous turn as she became a celebrity interviewer and got a spot on a successful Italian TV comedy show called *L'Altra domenica*. In 1979 she acted in her first film, *The Meadow*, for the Taviani brothers, not from any deep-seated desire to be an actress but out of admiration for the two directors. The film was poorly received and Rossellini herself criticised for being 'too green'. Upset by its failure, she decided to give up acting, in her own words 'refusing to be the cause of disaster to other directors I loved'.

Soon afterwards she began a highly successful career as a model – she would in the course of her modelling career appear on the cover of *Vogue* twenty-eight times. In 1983 she became the exclusive model for Lancôme cosmetics. Her contract gave Lancôme the right to veto any advertising she might be offered elsewhere and contained a morals clause; the agreement would be terminated if she were involved in any scandal. It was the sort of arrangement her mother would have been familiar with as a contract star in the forties, and, in an age which has seen models become the representatives of glamour that movie stars had once been, Rossellini was really following in her mother's footsteps.

If conscious of her parents' competing influence she had wished to find an identity of her own, she could hardly have done better than to appear in *Blue Velvet*, but it required considerable courage. She must have known that she not only risked the invocation of the morals clause in her contract with Lancôme, but also would be at the heart of the controversy that the film was bound to attract. The comment of the film critic and columnist Rex Reed that Ingrid Bergman 'must be turning over in her grave' was an example of what an easy target she made.

Isabella Rossellini never wore any make-up until her modelling contract required that she should do so in public. So she began to wear bright red lipstick in her everyday life, fearing than any more subtle colour would not be noticed. But if modelling forced a gulf between her public and private self, it also left her peculiarly equipped to portray Dorothy's flight from reality, as she hides herself beneath a wig and make-up and in the **costumes** and stage lights of **the Slow Club**.

Her performance has the power of something un-actresslike and genuine. In playing Dorothy she drew on her own experience:

> I went deep inside me, into the confusion, fear and helplessness I had felt in eliciting sexual desire and attraction when I had been a beautiful young girl. I summoned up my memory of the trauma of date rape I had experienced and even a mysterious firmament that had appeared to me once when I had been brutally beaten. I had felt no pain, just total surprise . . . When I played Dorothy, asking to be beaten, I recalled those stars. The way of stopping the anguished thoughts – 'the clouds' – was to be hit and be bewildered in front of this firmament.

S

Sandy

The first time Jeffrey sees Sandy is when she emerges out of the darkness as he leaves the Williams's house. 'You're the person who found **the ear**,' she says to him. Her knowledge is intuitive. When Jeffrey asks her how she knows, she replies: 'I just know. That's all.' Sandy tells him what she's learnt about the severed ear. As they stroll through the night-time streets together, she dangles bits of information before him like bait. She tells him about Dorothy Vallens and offers to show him where she lives.

It's a courtship without her even knowing, an instinctive thing. 'C'mon,' she says seductively, as she takes Jeffrey to see the building. She has no idea where it will lead, but something about Jeffrey is drawing her on, just as later something about Dorothy will draw Jeffrey on. There's a brightness in her eyes as she shows him the building. She finds it thrilling.

Sandy is as **voyeuristic** as Jeffrey. She knows so much about the case because her room is above her father's office and she listens in on his conversations. She may warn Jeffrey about the dangers of sneaking into Dorothy's apartment, but nonetheless she's eager to learn what he's seen. When Jeffrey shows her father the photographs he's taken of Frank and the Yellow Man she waits on the stairs outside her father's office, burning with curiosity. Her appetite never slackens. Even after Jeffrey has grown tired of the dangerous world he's found himself in, she continues to question him about things.

But Sandy's so innocent that even drinking beer seems a novelty to her. When Jeffrey takes her to **the Slow Club** to watch Dorothy's act, he buys a couple of Heinekens. Their conversation suggests the childhood limits of her world.

'Man, I like Heineken,' says Jeffrey. 'You like Heineken?'
'Well, I've never really had Heineken before,' she replies awkwardly.
'You've never had Heineken before?'
'My dad drinks Bud.'

Sandy longs to venture beyond the shelter of her upbringing. Her father's overprotective, yet she accepts his role as the authority figure in her life. She is curious, but prudent. Her chief objection to Jeffrey sneaking into Dorothy's apartment is its recklessness. Her maturity contrasts with Jeffrey's lack of it. While Jeffrey is unable to temper his curiosity, Sandy always manages to keep hers in harness. When Jeffrey keeps quiet about his discovery that her father's partner Detective Gordon is working for Frank, she knows he's hiding something from her but accepts that that's the way it has to be.

Sandy finds Jeffrey both attractive and frightening. When she agrees to break a date with her boyfriend Mike to go with Jeffrey to the Slow Club, she adds: 'Just so the record's kept straight, though, I love Mike.' But it's a profession of love that is hard to take very seriously. There's something automatic and unconsidered about it – more a hanging on to the secure, predictable world that Mike represents. When Jeffrey kisses her for the first time she tells him not to, although it is clear that she is falling in love with him. Again, it is an instinct for security.

That the all-American football-playing Mike does not suit her is obvious from the poster on her bedroom wall. Not some **eighties** icon like Harrison Ford, but Montgomery Clift, the **fifties** Hollywood star with a dark **secret**. Sandy is attracted to people with hidden depths. It is natural that she should find herself increasingly drawn to Jeffrey with his appetite for mystery and his sense of the strangeness of the world. She is a young girl in the process of becoming a woman. She is waking up, casting aside the received ideas of her childhood and beginning to think for herself.

She is the strongest and most impressive character in the film. Jeffrey may be the more adventurous in the actual pursuit of knowledge, but in its attainment Sandy's intuition keeps her far ahead. When Jeffrey is on the point of despair after what he has witnessed in **Deep River Apartments** it is Sandy who fortifies him by telling him about her dream:

> There was our world, and the world was dark because there weren't any **robins**. And the robins represented love, and for the longest time there was just the **darkness**. And all of a sudden thousands of robins were set free and they flew down and brought this blinding light of love and it seemed like that love would be the only thing that would make any difference. And it did.

These words are kitsch, but moving because they are spoken with such sincerity, and by a young person who we would not normally expect to have thought so deeply about such things.

Sandy represents a harmony. She is curious but careful. She prefers the safety of home, yet in the appropriate circumstances is prepared to risk extreme danger. When in the film's finale she has trouble getting hold of her father to go to Jeffrey's rescue, she rushes over to Deep River Apartments herself. At last she ventures beyond the protection of her father and takes her life into her own hands. Perhaps that's her lesson – that true love is worth taking extreme risks for.

She knows how to temper her emotions with reason. When she learns the truth of Jeffrey's involvement with Dorothy she slaps him across the cheek in her anger, but later, remembering her dream and that 'love would be the only thing that would make any difference', she quickly forgives him. In the most heated situations she never forgets her concern for others. 'Watch out for Mike,' she says to Jeffrey as they leave Jeffrey's house in a hurry. And she asks after Dorothy only hours after learning how she has been betrayed.

Sandy is the most fully realised depiction of human goodness to be found in *Blue Velvet*. It was only with the recent rerelease of that other fifties nostalgia movie, *Grease*, that I realised where I'd seen her before – the pure and virginal and 'hopelessly devoted' Sandy Olsen (Olivia Newton-John) trying with great difficulty at high school to recapture her summer romance with tough guy Danny Zuko (John Travolta).

See **Dern, Laura; duck, the**.

secrets

Everybody has a secret in *Blue Velvet*. It's as basic a fact of life as money or **sex**. Detective Williams wants to keep his investigation secret. Dorothy hides a photograph of her husband, Don, and son under a sofa and calls Jeffrey her 'secret lover'. Sandy tells her schoolfriends not to tell her boyfriend Mike about Jeffrey, who in this respect is her secret lover too. The Yellow Man's secret is that he's a corrupt cop. Even the appallingly frank Frank has a secret. For all his bravado, his bragging of his strength, he is impotent.

And Jeffrey, for whom it's such a thrill to be in the middle of 'something that was always hidden', is as adept at hiding secrets as he is at revealing them. He can tell Sandy about Frank and Dorothy, but not reveal the full truth about his own part in the story. He can tell Detective Williams about what he has found out, but keep quiet about Sandy's involvement.

severed ear

See **ear, the**.

710

In **Deep River Apartments**, where Dorothy lives, everything about the building suggests her degradation and breakdown. In the lobby faulty electric connections fizz and visitors have to take the stairs because the elevator doesn't work. Poor Dorothy is not someone you can get through to easily. As Jeffrey climbs the stairs the building groans with a factory-like humming.

The apartment itself looks as if it's rotting. The bare, undecorated walls are a bloody purple and the floor a sort of shit colour. The settees, crude and lumpen slabs, are more like meat boards than furniture. On a mantelpiece there are two plants. They look like fungoid growths that need neither water nor sunlight but feed instead on the damp and the dry rot. This is a place where growth is stunted and nothing can possibly flower. The TV set is in a wooden box. On top, insect-like and intrusive – like a Big Brother monitoring device – sits a primitive, two-pronged aerial. It makes you question Dorothy's reception. You feel that such a device could not possibly deliver the programmes that the rest of **America** is getting, but instead something from the outer limits.

With its spartan, white-painted cupboards, which must date back to **the fifties** or earlier, the kitchen is yet another sign of neglect. When Jeffrey, disguised as a bugman, comes to spray it for cockroaches, Dorothy shows no surprise whatever at his appearance. Only creatures so hardy could thrive here. The overall impression is of somewhere stifling and toxic. Dorothy's apartment would be a challenge for any estate agent.

sex

Usually we contrive to ignore it, to go about our business as if it does not exist, but every now and then we are reminded of the extraordinary nether world of sex. Not the golden-fleshed clinches of primetime TV, but the mysterious, unexplored hinterland.

Iris, who lives in the next street along, was telling me about her **neighbour**. At about nine o'clock every Thursday evening a lady with a carpet bag would arrive at his front door. As the night wore on, Iris would then hear through her party wall orgasmic shrieks and what sounded like whips cracking. The rumpus kept her awake into the small hours. Then at about eight the next morning a car would arrive and take the lady and her bag away again. Her neighbour would emerge a few minutes later in a suit and with a briefcase under his arm.

Iris didn't like to say anything, but then one day, when she played her piano later into the night than she normally would, the neighbour knocked on her door and asked if she could keep the noise down.

'Well, we could all keep the noise down, couldn't we?' she replied indignantly.

This nether world challenges our notions of the 'normal' and the 'acceptable'. It's hidden but widespread. Our friends could belong to it; we could even slip into it ourselves. It's a world that evokes a simultaneous fascination and disgust. Some deep-seated sense of shame causes us to pass a veil over our own activities and to greet the accounts of what other people get up to with shocked disbelief or protective laughter.

We fear this nether world for its unruliness – worry that, allowed to bubble up to the surface, it might threaten the order necessary for the smooth functioning of our lives. We regard with suspicion even those who do no more than look upon it – it seems perverse to linger willingly on something so dangerous. *Blue Velvet* not only dares to look, but also captures our unease about such daring. 'I don't know whether you're a detective or a pervert,' Sandy says to Jeffrey. As the critic Pauline Kael pointed out, it's a sign of her naivety: 'She's still a kid; she thinks it's either/or.'

Whether as chief motivation or as symptom of something else, sex is at the heart of *Blue Velvet*. Not only do the main characters seem most readily explained in its terms, but it drives the **plot**: Frank kidnaps

Dorothy's son and cuts off her husband's **ear** to force her to be his sex slave. 'I'll fuck anything that moves!' is Frank's battle-cry. He hides a physical impotence behind a preposterous sexual bluff and sublimates his sexual urges in violence. He's like the all-powerful Wizard of Oz, who, once he comes out of his booth, is revealed to be a very, very little man indeed. There's something pathetic about the way he is for ever boasting about his prowess. 'Do you see, Ben? I can make him do anything I fuckin' please,' he says after forcing Jeffrey to drink a toast to his friend.

When, later, Frank beats Jeffrey up in **Meadow Lane**, it's like a rape. He smears lipstick all over Jeffrey's face and forces kisses on him. Dorothy, looking helplessly on, screams at him to stop. He then slowly wipes the lipstick off with his piece of blue velvet before finally beating him up. It's as close as Frank can get to the sexual act, and recalls the earlier scene in **Deep River Apartments** when Frank stuffs Dorothy's blue velvet gown into her mouth and up her vagina. The lipstick on Jeffrey's face looks like blood. He has lost his virginity.

Sex has the appeal for Lynch of being something simple yet impossibly complex, a primal urge which, however, manifests itself in an infinite number of forms. He's compared it to jazz – 'it can be the same tune, but there are many variations on it' – and spoken of it as 'the vast realm' that 'has all these different levels, from lust and fearful, violent sex to the real spiritual thing at the other end'.

Blue Velvet lingered on the destructive aspects of sex, but hinted at an alternative vision as, in its concluding stages, the 'mysteries of love come clear' for Jeffrey and Sandy. As if picking up on this cue, *Wild at Heart* articulated 'the real spiritual thing at the other end'. It depicted a young couple who were confused by life – 'wild at heart and weird on top' – but enjoyed a physical harmony. There was a purity; Lula's and Sailor's sexual pleasure mirrored a wider devotion. They had given themselves up to a relationship of total trust and loyalty.

Yet there was the dark counterpoint too – Sailor and Lula on the run from Lula's wicked witch of a mother, vengeful because Sailor has spurned her sexual advances. Such an Oedipal pull is a recurring theme in Lynch's films. In *Twin Peaks: Fire Walk with Me* the mystery of Laura Palmer has its source in a father's sexual abuse of his daughter. In *Blue Velvet* Jeffrey becomes a kind of surrogate child to Frank and Dorothy, sleeping with one and killing the other.

Whatever the nature of its manifestation, whether for good or evil, Lynch treats sex as a fundamental component of human behaviour – like the atomic particles in matter: 'It's the key to some fantastic mystery of life.' Usually suppressed by the routine and taboo of daily life, it is here that the conflicting forces within us find their most ready battleground.

Shostakovitch (1906–75)

Lynch listened to Shostakovitch's Symphony No. 15 in A Major while he wrote the script. He had intended that it should be used as the theme and **mood music** for the film, and a note to this effect prefaces the final draft. While he was directing the film, he listened to the music on a headset. When, finally, he decided that **Angelo Badalamenti** should do the score, he asked him if he could compose in the same style. '"Make it with a Russian flavour, very beautiful but a bit threatening,"' Badalamenti remembered Lynch saying. 'It's a generalisation, yet specific at the same time. I just had to sit down and do it. Luckily it was not a problem.'

★　　★　　★

sickest film ever made?

The American critic Rex Reed described *Blue Velvet* as 'one of the sickest films ever made'. Pauline Kael prefaced her *New Yorker* review with these words, overheard after a showing of the film: 'Maybe I'm sick, but I want to see that again.'

Blue Velvet was not one of those films that hid its light under a bushel; it set the bushel ablaze. Whether you liked it or not, the film was impossible to dismiss. As Pauline Kael put it: 'When you come out of the theatre after seeing David Lynch's *Blue Velvet*, you certainly know that you've seen something.' There was a delicious ambivalence in the critics' response that mirrored the film's own **dualistic** nature. The *Daily Telegraph* wrote: 'It is insidiously subversive and utterly fascinating.' *The New York Times* said: 'It confirms Mr Lynch's stature as an innovator, a superb technician, and someone best not encounterered in a dark alley.'

If few disputed the film's technical brilliance, many questioned its morality. 'What Lynch shows us with Dorothy,' wrote Geoff Andrew in *Time Out*, 'is a woman so brutalised by Frank's incessant beatings and insults that she actively desires to be hurt by whoever she meets; only with physical and mental cruelty is love possible.' He went on: 'It is indeed both on a technical and an artistic level an often amazing, memorable achievement. But, morally, it's more complicated than that. A lot of women, for example, will be deeply upset by some of the scenes . . . that focus unflinchingly on Frank's humiliation of Dorothy; even more will shudder at the sight of her begging Jeffrey, repeatedly, to hurt her. And if the reply comes that all this is psychologically explicable, one might also remember that these scenes of torment and degradation are being held up as *spectacle*, something to enjoy.'

Not that he thought such behaviour *was* psychologically explicable, as the heavily rhetorical questions that peppered the last paragraphs of the article made plain: 'Is this what we as men and women are really

about? Or is this merely the fevered product of Lynch's imagination? . . .
Are these fantasies healthy? Is it healthy that we should take uncritical
enjoyment from observing them?' And he concluded: 'Originality and
genius, after all, are not everything; a little honesty, a little moral
awareness are also worth bearing in mind.'

The reviewer for the *New Statesman* – another man – adopted a
similar stance, although he found few compensating pleasures to temper
his condemnation:

> The view of sexuality imparted in *Blue Velvet* – in particular that
> of a woman whose pleasure is dependent upon being physically
> beaten – is loathsome and grossly **misogynistic**. That a woman
> who has just been raped should urge a **voyeuristic** intruder
> out of the wardrobe and wish him upon her violated body is
> a fantasy of similar proportions. It adds to a general catalogue
> of representations within which women's bodies, commodified
> and packaged by men, are offered for male consumption.

Behind such attitudes of reproval lies a failure of imagination, an
unwillingness to contemplate the extremes to which human beings
can be driven. Dorothy's behaviour is far more complex than their
representation of it. Her desires are contradictory – she wants both to
be hurt and not to be hurt. Her conduct is driven by a suicidal despair.
'I think she wants to die,' Jeffrey confides to Sandy. In the appalling state
that Frank has reduced her to, her personality comes apart. There's a
desperate pathos to her situation, which Lynch portrays with a sympathy
that makes accusations of misogyny seem extraordinary. To depict
cruelty is not to be cruel.

Both pieces criticised Lynch as if he were making some statement
about women in general. But although Dorothy's story is certainly
the focus, the overall impression *Blue Velvet* gives is one of the
infinite variety of human experience: 'It's a strange world.' Also,

Sandy is as positive an example of womanhood as Dorothy is an unhappy one.

The incredulity of some of the critics corresponds to an attitude that is represented in the film. The grown-ups either bury or fail to accept outlandish things beyond their own experience. 'I don't see how they do it,' says Aunt Barbara, as with Sandy and Jeffrey she looks at a **robin** eating an insect. 'I could never eat a bug.' *Blue Velvet* dared to look at unpleasant truths which society prefers not to confront. Far from offering up 'scenes of torment and degradation' as spectacle and enjoyment, it was actually a very rare example of a film-maker seeking first and foremost, like a true artist, to provide a vision of reality. Few people would find the scenes of Dorothy's degradation in **Deep River Apartments** enjoyable at all.

A little to my surprise, the reviews I came across that were written by women were far more tolerant and understanding of these scenes. Angela Brooks, in *Today*, wrote: 'It's harrowing stuff, that has earned it epithets of "porn" in some quarters. I disagree. It neither titillates, glories nor exonerates and, as such, towers above the dross – while still grazing the very belly of hell.' Similarly, Virginia Dignam observed: '*Blue Velvet* is not an exploitation film. It peels away the many skins of the onion to find what is hidden at the heart. As a sharp observer of the darker side of life, Lynch takes a tough look at sex and sexism and dismisses many cherished beliefs and stereotypes.' On the other side of the Atlantic, Pauline Kael, in *The New Yorker*, Janet Maslin of *The New York Times* and Lizzie Borden of *The Village Voice* all wrote admiringly of the film.

With hindsight, perhaps the most startling criticism came from the novelist Barry Gifford: 'This is an ugly, brutal, but naive movie. One cut above a snuff film. A kind of academic porn. It's interesting to me that I can never imagine things as depraved as those that occur here, and I've always thought I could get pretty low in that department. Pornography, as such, simply bores me; as soon as I know what it is I lose interest.'

Like Jeffrey discovering that he had more in common with Frank than he thought, Gifford would end up working with Lynch. *Wild at Heart* was based on his novel, and the two wrote together the script of Lynch's film *Lost Highway*.

See **therapy**.

sincerest form of flattery

It's when you try to think of Lynch's imitators that he seems most a one-off. *Blue Velvet* belonged to a wave of mid-**eighties** films, such as *True Stories*, *Peggy Sue Got Married* and *River's Edge*, that re-evaluated the idyll of small-town **America**. But what made it stand out as unique was its surreal, hallucinogenic effect. Arguably, Dennis Hopper as Frank unleashed a renewed interest in the kinks of the criminal mind – one thinks of Hannibal Lecter in *The Silence of the Lambs*, the vicious moral crusader John Doe in *Seven*, even the sociopath Bridget Gregory in *The Last Seduction* – but such larger-than-life villains have never been in short supply.

Blue Velvet's most lasting effect was an indirect one – as the father of *Twin Peaks*. Although the film had enjoyed notoriety, few people actually saw it. In contrast, the *Twin Peaks* TV series attracted a huge television audience and shifted perceptions of what a mainstream audience would watch. Its commercial success led to a tidal wave of exercises in the quirky and the bizarre. Lynch must probably be held accountable for the notion of hidden forces at work ('Things are not what they seem') that has so dominated the TV schedules of the 1990s. King of the imitators has been the *X-Files* (David Duchovny's first taste of the paranormal was playing a transvestite FBI agent in *Twin Peaks*). But *Northern Exposure*, *Due South*, *Wild Palms* and *American Gothic* all owe a debt.

★   ★   ★

Slow Club, the

It's a place where you can sit down and unwind, a place to lose yourself in dreams, the kind of place where Frank would conduct a lot of his **drugs** business. One night, I imagine, after all the deals had been done, he stopped for a **Pabst Blue Ribbon** or two, and there was this new act, a foreign girl singing a song he remembered from more simple times. And the deep-blue velvet robe she wore brought back some long-lost maternal embrace. Far gone with drugs and alcohol – and in any case naturally emotional – he was bewitched by **the Blue Lady**.

He sensed her vulnerability, but also her need to give unreservedly. It corresponded perfectly with his own need to possess, and to overwhelm. He had to have her. When he got to her dressing room, he found her husband and son. But for someone like Frank that was more an opportunity than an obstacle, the means to force her to comply with his will.

sound

It is a sound that first intimates disaster. We see Jeffrey's father Mr Beaumont watering his lawn. There's a cut from Mr Beaumont to the connection of the hose with the tap. We hear a hissing of water escaping from the connection and a fierce, slightly metallic juddering sound as if a washer has worked loose. But the brilliance of the scene lies in the counterpoint of sound and image.

Mr Beaumont tries to free a length of hose but it becomes snagged on the branch of a bush. We hear a brushing sound. As he checks the water flow, there's a cut back to the tap. The juddering is now in full momentum, its demonic tone threatening an imminent explosion. There's a cut to the hosepipe snagged on the branch. We hear a brushing sound again as Mr Beaumont tugs at the hose. There's a cut back to the tap and the juddering sound, then there's a cut of image only to Mr Beaumont having his seizure, while the fearsome juddering continues. There's a violence in this sudden disjunction of sound and image. It brings home the metaphor. Mr Beaumont has blown a gasket. And all the while in the background – the bridge between the serene and the sinister – we hear Bobby Vinton singing 'Blue Velvet'.

It's one of those virtuoso sequences that film schools should put on a continuous loop for the benefit of their students, a demonstration of how sound is as integral a part of cinema as the image.

John Ross, the sound engineer who worked with David Lynch on the film *Lost Highway*, said of him, 'He's definitely not a "See a dog, hear a dog" kind of guy. He's more, "See a dog and possibly imagine what the dog is thinking."' At the heart of Lynch's film-making is the articulation of the intangible. It's **mood** and feeling that he seeks to capture rather than objective reality. Sound is a key tool in achieving this, whether **music** or sound effects. Indeed there's no logical distinction between the two, and they merge imperceptibly into each other. When Jeffrey visits **Deep River Apartments** for the first time, the machine-like humming of the building is punctuated intermittently by an almost musical chiming sound. When Jeffrey discovers **the ear** there's a very faint but unsettling background noise. It sounds a bit like unseen insects buzzing away, but also like the gentle rolling of drums or symbols. Mixed in, barely audible, are several more sounds impossible to identify. Whether in these sequences we hear music or sound effects is really immaterial. It's certainly not something that you're meant to analyse or even be conscious of. It's there without you realising. It sets a tone but defies explanation, just like a mood.

See **Splet, Alan R**.

Splet, Alan R. (1939–94)

One of Lynch's oldest **collaborators**. The two first worked together on *The Grandmother* in 1970, and the partnership continued until Splet's death from cancer in 1994. On *The Grandmother* they spent sixty-three days recording effects. Splet had suggested that they should look for their own after nothing suitable could be found on **sound** effects records. 'The trick is finding the right sound to make the mood go hand in hand with the picture,' Lynch has said. 'Only a couple of sounds are right when millions and millions are wrong.' Splet possessed the necessary combination of sensitivity and thoroughness. He was prepared to travel the world for the appropriate sound, and to experiment endlessly.

Jeffrey hitting Dorothy is one of the most disturbing punches in movie history. It owed much to Splet's perfectionism. Not satisfied with the sound of a regular punch, he re-recorded it at half speed, and then laid the normal speed and half-speed punches together. Finally, as one of Splet's assistants on the film recalled, 'we hit a big, old dried-out pumpkin with an 18-inch cork-backed steel ruler. We just slapped it, which gave an incredible, really vicious, whipping noise. . . . Mixing these three sounds together, we ended up with a violent punch.'

Just as much effort went into creating sounds that the audience wouldn't consciously notice, but which nonetheless created an ambience. 'A good soundtrack can heighten the whole story-telling process,' Splet commented. 'It's a way of having things work on people without them being too aware of it.'

When Jeffrey discovers the severed **ear**, a faint, barely audible susurration – you have to make a conscious effort to hear it – gives the scene its chilling atmosphere, the sense of the untoward suddenly cropping up amidst the normal. To achieve it, Splet stretched a thin layer of latex rubber over a bucket of cockroaches. 'Then we turned the bucket over, and, of course, as soon as the roaches hit the latex they went scurrying like crazy. So we got this sound of little insect feet running all over the rubber.' The sound was then speeded up in order to thin it out.

Splet's achievement as a pioneer in the creative use of sound was acknowledged by the Academy of Motion Picture Sciences when he received a Special Achievement **Oscar** in 1979 for his work on *The Black Stallion.*

Splet suffered from impaired vision but, as Lynch commented, 'when you have one sense impaired, others jump up. Al could hear things that others couldn't.' The blind half of Double Ed who works in the Beaumont's hardware store seems like a tribute. He knows how many fingers Jeffrey is holding up although he can't see them.

Stewart, James (1908–97)

It was a shock to see *Vertigo* again recently. I had forgotten that James Stewart had ever played so disturbed and cruel a character. He's a mental wreck in a sanatorium unable even to recognise his closest friend, then he's a pitiless Pygmalion forcing Kim Novak to dress as the dead woman he had loved. It's much easier to remember him as the crusading Scout Master in *Mr Smith Goes to Washington* or as George Bailey in *It's a Wonderful Life*, doing good in his home town of Bedford Falls when he would much rather have travelled the world. It fits in more comfortably with the details of his own life – the happily married man who made his acting debut in a Boy Scout play and flew twenty missions over wartime Germany. Two movie traditions war within his screen persona – Capra's small town idealist and Hitchcock's disillusioned obsessive.

In *Blue Velvet* his spiritual presence is strong. It's there in the often remarked upon resemblances with one-time Eagle Scout David Lynch, whom Mel Brooks perceptively dubbed a 'Jimmy Stewart from Mars'. It's there too in a narrative that seems, whether consciously or otherwise, to merge the storylines of three classic Stewart movies. And it's there in the way Capra's Stewart and Hitchcock's merge in Jeffrey, who has all the naivety of the one and the tendency to infatuation of the other. As the archetypal example of the regular guy with a dark side, I can picture him – or rather his ghost – looking on as Jeffrey looks on, fascinated like the photographer in **Rear Window** but also benignly concerned like Clarence the guardian angel in *It's a Wonderful Life*.

See **MacLachlan, Kyle**.

Stockwell, Dean (b. 1936)

'When I first read the script,' Stockwell recalled, 'here was Dennis's character, Frank Booth, so unforgettably black and psychologically villainous. And now he's going to visit *my* character, who is someone that he looks up to. It occurred to me that this Ben had to be fucking stranger than Frank.'

Frank may be the beast, but it's Ben who calls the tune. Camp and decadent, his oddity has a showbusiness charm, his painted face resembling the MC in *Cabaret*. Dean Stockwell came from a showbusiness family. His mother, Betty Veronica Stockwell, appeared in *Oklahoma!* on the Broadway stage and his father, Harry Stockwell, was the voice of Prince Charming in Disney's *Snow White and the Seven Dwarfs* (Dean lip-synching Roy Orbison's 'In Dreams' makes a satisfying full circle). He made his movie debut at the age of seven, with Gene Kelly and Frank Sinatra in *Anchors Aweigh!*

Making Ben strange came naturally to Stockwell, because his own life had been pretty strange. He has spoken in interviews of feeling like a freak when he was a child star in Hollywood. In Joseph Losey's *The Boy with Green Hair* he played a war orphan who is victimised when his hair mysteriously turns green. 'I want to be like everybody else!' the boy cries.

In his attempts to become like everybody else Stockwell would spend much of his life travelling in the opposite direction. While everybody else in Los Angeles was dreaming of becoming a star, Stockwell was trying to get away from the town. When he was 16 he left Hollywood and drifted around **America**, taking up odd jobs under a false name. But five years later, fit for nothing else, he was back acting in the movies again. In the seventies, he moved to Santa Fe, New Mexico, with the ambition of earning a living in real estate. But suddenly he found himself being offered a series of films too good to refuse: Wim Wenders' *Paris, Texas*; William Friedkin's *To Live and Die in LA*; Lynch's **Dune**.

As happy as he was to leave showbusiness life behind, it always seemed to be waiting for him round the corner. If Ben is bizarre but cosy, the workaday movie star knew how these qualities need not be in contradiction.

Playing Ben revitalised Stockwell's career. He would win an **Oscar** nomination for his role as the mob boss Tony 'the Tiger' Russo in Jonathan Demme's *Married to the Mob*. Demme commented on the 'flamboyant, debonair quality' of the character, 'the perverted sense of style'. And he appeared as Rear-Admiral Albert Calavicci in the successful TV series *Quantum Leap*, winning a Golden Globe Award for Best Supporting Actor. Other film appearances include *Tucker: The Man and His Dream*, *Sandino*, *The Player*, *Chasers*, *Airforce One* and the *Rainmaker*.

Stovitz, Ken

See **Mike**.

T

texture

If the film's title is not a sufficient indication, its very first images make Lynch's love of texture clear: the blue velvet material against which the opening credits roll, the deep blue sky which follows, the hypnotic supersaturated tulips and roses against the white picket fence. Nothing just *happens* to be before the camera, but everything, whether beautiful or ugly, is dwelt upon with an artist's fascination. It's like a garden by Capability Brown – artfully arranged nature.

In *Blue Velvet* there's an intensity of perception, a looking for its own sake, that reaches beyond the surface of things. This compulsion to see has its unsavoury aspect, relishing, as it does, the bad every bit as much the good. When Lynch depicts Jeffrey's father's seizure he seems to find something awe-inspiring and wonderful about the process – it's as if he were witnessing a natural disaster like a volcano exploding. His camera lingers lovingly over the calamity. You feel that if he were on the scene his first words would not be 'Better call an ambulance', but 'Wow! That was extraordinary'. There's an exhilaration in capturing what normally cannot be seen. As Mr Beaumont lies prostrate on the ground the camera slows down the gouts of water spraying from the hose, as if too fascinated to let go of the image and determined to discover its constituent parts. It's a voyeur's instinct, but also a key to understanding.

Lynch uses texture, like **sound** and **music**, to convey **mood**. It is a way of getting under the skin of the characters. The pattern of the

trees under which Jeffrey and Sandy walk in the night-time streets
conveys the mysteriousness of the world they are entering. The
oppressive detail of Dorothy's apartment, with its pools of darkness,
or Mr Beaumont's water supply cut off by a snagged hosepipe provides
an outward representation of an inner process.

therapy

I rang up Bernie Wooder, the movie therapist. A psychotherapist of
eleven years' standing, he is the only practitioner registered with the
United Kingdom Council of Psychotherapists to use films regularly
in his work. There had been articles in the papers about him. MGM
had reissued their *Wizard of Oz* video with his endorsement of its
therapeutic value. What, I wondered, would he make of *Blue Velvet*?
Could he ever imagine endorsing this story of an infinitely more
troubled Dorothy?

Bernie explained that the newspaper articles had been misleading.
Contrary to what they had suggested, it was not his practice to
recommend films. He preferred it when patients already had something
in mind, and would only suggest a particular film when he had come to
know someone very well.

Inevitably, most of the films he talked about with his patients
were mainstream Hollywood ones, with their implicit assumption
of an ordered world. But he admired *Blue Velvet* for its courage in
acknowledging the disturbing side. 'In fact I would go so far as to say
what Lynch does is to reverse things and make disturbing features the
star of his films. He doesn't make the star the star. He makes what's
disturbing the star.' It reminded him of the ending of *Bonnie and Clyde*,
where the camera lingers in slow motion over the bullet-riddled death
throes of the two outlaws. 'The cleverness was showing in that balletic
way the ugliness of violence – it didn't make it acceptable, like cowboys
– and I think Lynch does the same thing.'

He could understand why many people would turn away from *Blue Velvet*, but he thought it could have a therapeutic value for those who were able to face up to its disturbing nature. It offered so many models of behaviour with which to help them gain an insight into the troubled areas of their lives. He could imagine it being particularly useful to people who had been involved in unhealthy relationships. Jeffrey was an example of someone who is pulled into a dangerous relationship but then, having discovered his 'shadow' side, succeeds in breaking away and regaining a healthy equilibrium.

He offered this insight into Dorothy's situation: when victims of rape describe what they have suffered, they often relate it as though it had happened to someone else. They distance themselves from the pain of their feelings. Dorothy had so numbed herself in this way that she came to long to be hurt in order to feel emotion again.

Bernie was impressed by how many different perspectives the film offered. Not just the destructive world of Frank and Dorothy, but also the rites of passage of Jeffrey, and the example of nourishing love and trust that Sandy provides. Lynch 'balances out' he said; he gives a very real, albeit idyllic, picture of contented domestic bliss and love, but does not ignore the ugly.

It made Bernie think of Berchtesgaden – the wolf's lair: 'I don't know whether you've ever been there, but it's beautiful.' Here in a picture postcard paradise Hitler orchestrated the murder of millions. It was this sharp contrast in man's nature that Lynch captured so perfectly.

We went on to talk about Frank – an easy step in the conversation. 'He's psychotic and very dangerous and the **drugs** don't help him.' He reminded Bernie of Jekyll and Hyde. Dr Jekyll is a gentle man who starts to drink his own potion. It releases in him his animalistic, shadow side. At first he's able to return to being Jekyll again, but gradually the effects of the potion become so strong that his unconscious gets out of control and takes him over. Frank has his well-dressed man disguise, but it's hard to imagine that he could ever have been a *gentle* man. He's too lost in the 'shadow' side to find its opposite. But occasionally there are flickerings of another self. There's the soothing effect that Ben has on him, and the songs he listens to. For brief moments he can let himself go and dream.

Usually when I admit that, for all his evil, my heart goes out to Frank, people look at me as if I'm as dangerous a nutcase as he is. But I knew that Bernie – who, after all, has to think about such things for a living – would understand: 'Yes, because he's living in hell, isn't he? The drugs numb him from a personal hell. He's in the grip of such chaos that he's like a ship without a rudder, at the mercy of any **mood** swing that might take him.'

Frank knows he's not healthy, but it's just too painful for him to come to terms with it. 'Don't look at me,' he screams at Dorothy as he belts her. This is shocking, brutal, but full of pathos too. For as he degrades Dorothy, so he degrades himself, and he can't tolerate that anyone should bear witness to such frailty. Poor old Frank! But I didn't ask, 'What do you think you could do for him, Bernie?' because I knew the answer. Frank's the therapist's nightmare. The key to therapy is awareness, which Frank actively shuns. You have to want to be cured.

I told Bernie how Lynch had once considered being psychoanalysed but decided not to in case it might affect his creativity. 'I'm sure it would,' he replied, 'because, quite simply, his art is his therapy.' Some people, he thought, have found a way of doing their own therapy – artists usually have.

See **misogyny**; **sickest film ever made?**; **voyeurism**.

This is It

The name of the bar to which Frank and his **gang** take Jeffrey, and where Ben has his apartment. The gang stand outside the building while Frank sorts out what beers everyone's having, but end up in Ben's place without us ever seeing the bar itself. In the script the bar was called the Barbary Coast and footage was shot inside that was left out of the finished film.

In the cut sequence, as a black man sings blues songs, Frank goes up to a man called Willard, who is surrounded by a group of naked girls, and throws him down on a pool table. He takes him to task for a scuffle in which his pocket got torn, causing him to lose his 'lucky piece of blue velvet'. Frank says to the naked girls, 'Come here and take a look at a dead man,' and then goes up some stairs with his gang to Ben's place. As Paul passes by the pool table he says to Willard, 'See ya, Winky.' Once Frank and the gang have disappeared, Willard sits up, and one of the naked girls strikes a match and sets her nipples on fire, saying, 'You're really going up in flames this time, motherfucker!'

Lynch has described it as one of his favourite scenes, but cut it because it was 'too much of a good thing', distracting from what followed in Ben's apartment. It was an example of the sort of readjustment that his improvisatory approach to filming could require. The visit to Ben's took on a new dimension with the last-minute introduction of the Roy Orbison song 'In Dreams'. As Ben lip-synchs the words he seems to hold Frank under a spell. The scene had a hypnotic power that far exceeded the scripted version and made the preceding Willard episode redundant.

tooth, chipped

See **chipped tooth**.

twelve years on

Blue Velvet may have been the most talked about film of the **eighties**, but in box-office terms it was merely a modest film that did good but unexceptional business, way down the league of the top American grossers for 1986. It was made for $5 million, and total US box office receipts, as of February 1997, amounted to $8,551,228. Compare this to the $109,713,132 taken by a major studio film made at about the same time: *Star Trek IV: The Voyage Home*. In Britain the two films had their London opening in the same week. After eight weeks *The Voyage Home* had taken £2,685,654, *Blue Velvet* £521,782. It was successful among sophisticated metropolitan audiences, but not of general appeal. The extraordinary thing was that *Twin Peaks*, which borrowed so much from *Blue Velvet*, should then have been the mainstream success that it was. In April 1990 35 million Americans tuned in to the two-hour pilot, making it the most watched TV feature of the season. Lynch's next movie, *Wild at Heart*, which was released in the summer of 1990, having won the *Palme d'Or* at Cannes, grossed $14,560,247.

Since then – commercially – Lynch has suffered a steep downhill ride. During its second season – broadcast on ABC over the winter of 1990–1 – the *Twin Peaks* TV show plummeted to eighty-fifth in the ratings and the network duly axed it. The *Twin Peaks* movie, *Fire Walk with Me*, was panned by the critics and grossed only $4,160,247 in the US. Some people accused Lynch of trying to milk the success of the *Twin Peaks* TV series (*Time Out*, for example: 'The film's makers . . . appear to have made no attempt to conceal the cynicism that presumably motivated their desire to cash in on their TV success.') But really the trouble was, on the contrary, his refusal to do so. He had dared to be different. Recreating the torment of Laura Palmer's last days, and eschewing straightforward narrative in favour of **mood**, it was Lynch's most unrelenting study in **darkness**. It was painful to watch but touched by scenes of brilliance.

There was something rather valiant about his attempt to show an audience familiar with the quirky, humorous touches of the TV show that the mystery of Laura Palmer was in fact no laughing matter. But he had overestimated the wish of cinema audiences to be challenged. They would probably have been happier with the same old thing.

Lost Highway was every bit as abstract as *Fire Walk with Me* had been.

It had an oneiric, hallucinatory quality. The reviews were a mixture of baffflement and admiration, but at the box office it fared even worse than *Fire Walk with Me* had done. The film dropped out out of *Screen International*'s US box office chart after four weeks, having taken just $2,829,362.

I recently hired the film on video. There was an endless parade of trailers for the distributor's other releases of the season. Brightly lit and regular, they made the dark and languid *Lost Highway* seem lost in their company. Panned and scanned and squeezed into a TV format, the film that had haunted me in the cinema was sadly diminished at home. It seemed too strange for the crude mass-market system of film distribution to cope with. It belonged not to the movie houses and Blockbuster Video, but to an as yet to be invented cinema art gallery with a more discriminating set of patrons.

In many ways *Lost Highway* is Lynch's most adventurous and sophisticated film. Although it may lack the formal perfection of *Blue Velvet*, the extraordinary fidelity with which it captures states of mind far exceeds what Lynch has previously achieved. If *Blue Velvet* still seems by far the more significant, it was because it had borrowed too many of Hollywood's clothes to be ignored. It observed the rules and conventions even as it subverted them, while *Lost Highway* lived up to its name in going off track.

Blue Velvet was a small film made for a major producer after Lynch had already directed two mainstream Hollywood movies – **The Elephant Man** and **Dune**. The project that evolved in these circumstances was perfectly pitched between the mainstream and the personal. Its success set Lynch on a new uncompromising path.

If few people went to see *Lost Highway*, it was because Lynch's instinct to break new ground had simply left audiences behind. He has returned to the avant-garde film-making with which he began. Mel Brooks' description of him as 'Jimmy Stewart from Mars' is more than ever apposite. His movie career is perhaps best thought of as a comet,

briefly yielding to earth's gravitational pull before hurtling back into
outer space again.

Twin Peaks

The TV series *Twin Peaks* turned Lynch into a household name,
making him known to a new drawing-room audience, most of whom
would never have seen his films in the cinema. It feasted on the
themes which Lynch had first brought into focus with *Blue Velvet*:
the small-town setting; the nostalgic nods to **the fifties** (the sheriff's
called Harry Truman); the rites of passage of young people on the
verge of adulthood; and, above all, as the title made clear from the
outset, a **dualistic** world of innocence and evil.

In the opening credits we see two streams of a waterfall merge
into one. The central mystery revolves around Laura Palmer, the
high-school homecoming queen who is discovered to have a dark
side. But also many of the other characters – in what amounted to
an elaborate soap opera – seemed to be conceived as contrasting pairs.
So among the teenagers there was the pure Donna Hayward and the
mischievous Audrey Horne; there was the noble biker James Hurley
and the unruly captain of the football team Bobby Briggs. So Ed,
the man who runs the gas station, is unhappily married to the crazy
Nadine but in love with the normal Norma, the level-headed owner
of the diner.

Kyle MacLachlan, the amateur detective in *Blue Velvet*, grows up to
become a real one. As Special Agent Dale Cooper, he's much more
sure of himself than his younger counterpart was, but possesses the same
curiosity. When he arrives in town he bombards Sheriff Truman with
questions not only about the case but also about the wonderful new
world he's found himself in: 'Sheriff, what kind of fantastic trees have
you got growing around here?'

Donna Hayward, Laura Palmer's best friend at school, strongly resembles Sandy. She even has a 'bonehead boyfriend' called Mike whom she ditches for her classmate James Hurley, just as Sandy ditches her Mike for Jeffrey. And both the Mikes seek to take revenge on their rivals.

Even the landmarks are familiar. In place of **the Slow Club** and **the Blue Lady**, there's the Roadhouse with its resident singer, Julee Cruise. In place of Arlene's diner, there's the Double R. And of course, like **Lumberton**, Twin Peaks is a town surrounded by trees. Indeed, you're aware of this in a way you're not in *Blue Velvet*; although Jeffrey lives in a lumber town and you see an awful lot of logs, you never see the forest.

The demands of mainstream television imposed several limitations, but there were also opportunities. In *Blue Velvet* the dictates of **mood** and narrative caused Lynch to reduce several secondary characters to rather shadowy figures. But with a TV series he could give rein to his talent for quirky, inconsequential detail and characterisation. Sandy's boyfriend Mike hardly features at all in the final film of *Blue Velvet*, although in the original script there was a richer, humorous portrait of an obsessive, health-mad footballer. It was this kind of comic vignette that blossomed in *Twin Peaks* – indeed, there are traces of the Mike that Lynch cut out from *Blue Velvet*, not only in his namesake, but also in the obsessive fitness fanatic Nadine. *Twin Peaks* amounted to a delicious indulgence. Lynch was free to experiment and to try out ideas without the pressure of having to make something perfect. It was *Blue Velvet* at play.

V

Vallens, Dorothy

See **Dorothy**.

Van Gogh

Frank's nickname for Dorothy's one-eared husband, Don.

Vertigo

James Stewart plays Scottie, an ex-detective who is asked by an old friend to follow his wife, Madeleine, whose strange behaviour worries him. Scottie reluctantly agrees to take on the assignment. He discovers that Madeleine is haunted by the memory of her great-grandmother Carlotta Valdes. A Spanish girl from a mission south of San Francisco, Carlotta was found 'dancing and singing in cabaret' by a rich man who took her as his mistress. She bore him a child, and after some years he kept the child but discarded her. A local historian tells Scottie of the rejected Carlotta's fate: 'She became the sad Carlotta, alone in the great house, walking the streets alone, her clothes becoming old and patched and dirty, and the mad Carlotta, stopping people in the streets to ask where is my child, have you seen my child.'

If Dorothy Vallens should ever have chanced to watch *Vertigo* on her derelict old TV set in **Deep River Apartments** she, no less than Madeleine, would have recognised her own story – a foreign cabaret singer bereft and suicidal over the kidnap of her child. Even the names are similar – Valdes/Vallens.

Scottie prevents Madeleine from killing herself as her ancestor had done. But then he falls deeply in love with her and fails to prevent a second suicide attempt. Overwhelmed with grief and guilt, he has a nervous breakdown. After his recovery he sees by chance a woman who looks exactly like Madeleine, except her hair is brown instead of blonde. Her name is Judy Barton. Haunted by the resemblance, he asks Judy out. He gets her to dress in the same clothes as Madeleine, to dye her hair and wear it as Madeleine would have worn hers. Regardless of Judy's feelings, he refashions her in the image of a dead woman. But as he achieves the fulfilment of this necrophiliac fantasy, he discovers that Judy really is Madeleine, and that she was not his friend's wife but his mistress. Her feigned death was part of a scheme to murder the real wife in such a way that the deluded Scottie would testify to her suicide. It's this twist that gives *Vertigo* the formal semblance of the suspense thriller. It's far-fetched but it doesn't matter because the **plot** is so much in the background and the **mood** of the film is so overpowering. The friend's hoax might be the occasion for the story, but the substance of *Vertigo* is no more that than *Blue Velvet* is Jeffrey's investigation into the mystery of the severed **ear**.

Both films are about obsession. Indeed Scottie's feverish pursuit of Madeleine falls into two parts, one recalling Jeffrey's infatuation with Dorothy, and the other Frank's. In the first part Scottie investigates Madeleine and falls in love with her. As he spies on her from a distance and becomes increasingly fascinated by her he resembles Jeffrey being pulled into Dorothy's tortuous world. In the second part, after Madeleine's supposed suicide, Scottie relentlessly refashions Judy into the dead Madeleine's image. It's a ritual that has all the kinkiness and desperation of Frank's abuse of Dorothy in Deep River Apartments. 'The gentleman seems to know what he wants,' a saleswoman comments on Scottie's insistence that Judy wear clothes of his choosing –

words which could as well apply to Frank forcing Dorothy to wear the blue velvet dress, let alone his other very particular requirements. Both Scottie and Frank treat their women as fetish objects.

Both films have a **dualistic** framework. In *Blue Velvet* there's the fair Sandy and the dark-haired Dorothy, the representatives of the sacred and profane. In *Vertigo* Kim Novak embodies these opposing qualities: there's the blonde Madeleine and the brunette Judy, one high class, the other low class. *Twin Peaks*, appropriately enough, offers an overt nod to such twinning. The blonde Laura Palmer has a dark-haired cousin called Maddie, who is her spitting image; and the two characters are played by the same actress, Sheryl Lee.

The two films also share a mirror-like narrative. *Blue Velvet* begins as it ends; in the second half the behaviour of a more experienced Jeffrey counterpoints that of the innocent Jeffrey in the first. Similarly, the second half of *Vertigo* repeats the first, as Scottie revisits Madeleine's old haunts. The whole logic of the narrative revolves around the illusion of the mirror image. Scottie finally discovers that 'Madeleine' and 'Judy' are different facets of the same person, just as he too embodies different selves: there's the sane, brave detective he used to be before he suffered his vertigo, and the vulnerable delusion-prone person he has become since. It's apt that he also should have two names. Old friends know him as John, he tells Madeleine, while acquaintances call him Scottie. In *Blue Velvet* Jeffrey discovers another side to his character, and Dorothy calls him by another name, Don.

While one should always be wary of assuming conscious imitation, the influence of *Vertigo* on *Blue Velvet* seems to me to be profound. The narrative resemblances are obvious, but the affinity is most of all one of **texture** and mood. Both directors push cinema to its limits in order to capture subjective states of mind. In *Vertigo* there's the famous kiss in the Empire Hotel. Judy has done up her hair so that finally she looks the exact image of the dead Madeleine. A neon light from the street outside bathes the bedroom in green. As she emerges from the bathroom, she looks at first like a ghostly apparition. As Stewart embraces her, the audience for a moment shares his sense of having snatched Madeleine back from death. The kiss lasts an age. The room revolves slowly around them and they seem to float free of earthly dimensions – for a brief moment, in his mind Scottie is back in the past, in the place where he last kissed Madeleine. There's a transcendant feeling of fulfilment, but also a disturbing, hallucinatory quality, for this kiss is a surrender to delusion.

Lynch achieves a similar degree of romantic intensity when Jeffrey and Sandy kiss at a party. They embrace and the camera holds them in close-up – as in *Vertigo*, isolating them from their background. It's more simply done and, I think, rings truer.

There's an irresistible grandeur about *Vertigo*, but also a vulgarity. It lives up to its name, in a vertiginous progress teetering on the edge of ludicrousness. Ladles of treacle are required to make the audience swallow the incongruity between the ethereal Madeleine and the earthy Judy. It's a dreamlike but massively implausible world, held together by the intensity of Scottie's obsession and the director's personal identification with it.

Hitchcock made deliciously rich fruitcakes of movies. His sense of what cinema could do was unparalleled, but his boldness could result in garishness. A nightmare after Madeleine's suicide signals Scottie's nervous breakdown. The director uses every trick from the manipulation of colour to animation to convey its fantasmagoric quality. But when a cut-out face of Scottie appears against a kaleidoscopic background or when his cut-out figure tumbles through the sky, as if Madeleine's suicide were his own, the effect is more comic book than true, brilliant but as over the top as a Rachmaninov concerto. No one could possibly mistake it for a real dream. On the other hand, Jeffrey's nightmares in *Blue Velvet* – expressed in brief, distorted images – are unnervingly lifelike.

Vertigo conveys the nature of a man's obsession with extraordinary intensity but offers little insight into anything else. *Blue Velvet*, in contrast, is a multilayered allegorical inquiry into the human condition. If it seems to me the greater of the two films, it's because it has a brilliance yet never sacrifices truth for effect. Content stands up to style.

voyeurism

After making **The Elephant Man** Lynch discussed his *Blue Velvet* idea with the producer Richard Roth: 'I told him I had always wanted to sneak into a girl's room to watch her at night and that, maybe, at one point or another, I would see something that would be a clue to a murder mystery.' In the finished film it would happen the other way round. Jeffrey discovers a clue to a murder mystery and then sneaks into a girl's room at night. It makes his voyeurism more palatable, because there is at least a semblance of a more worthwhile motive.

But the lingering fascination with which the worst excesses of human behaviour are depicted still led many people to speak of the film as 'sick'. There's a widespread assumption that just to look at such things is somehow unhealthy. The film alludes to this attitude with Sandy's query as to whether Jeffrey is a 'detective or a pervert'. Certainly what he witnesses through the crack in Dorothy's cupboard arouses a **sexual** interest that contributes nothing to his supposed investigation, but in driving him to confront his deepest instincts this voyeurism is shown to be vital. It is how he learns about himself. His discovery of the destructive side of his nature is the first step to controlling it.

Lynch's original idea of a person who at first indulges in voyeurism for its own sake can be found in the script of *Blue Velvet*. There, after Mr Beaumont has had his stroke, Mrs Beaumont telephones Jeffrey at college. His girlfriend, Louise, answers the call. He is nowhere to be found because he's hiding in a furnace room, spying on a student who, it soon becomes clear, is attempting to rape his girlfriend. Jeffrey intervenes: 'Hey, shit head. Leave her alone. Don't force girls!'

Lynch might as well have had him wear a college jersey with the word 'PERVERT' written on it. He becomes much more disturbing once his peeping is given a plausible pretext, because then we, the audience, become implicated in what he sees, and there is a sense of *normal* people being susceptible to dark forces.

See **misogyny**; *Rear Window*; **sickest film ever made**; **therapy**.

vox populi

'It's very dark,' said my brother Andrew. 'There's nothing joyous or happy about it. It's just very troubled.' It was Christmas day. While the rest of the family sat down after dinner to watch *Kind Hearts and Coronets*, we had turned on the small TV and the video upstairs. Andrew had heard I was writing a book and wanted to know what it was about. 'It says a lot about the mind of the person who made it,' he commented as the end credits rolled. 'If you got landed with this person at a party, you'd want to get away pretty quickly.'

Several times in the course of the film he pointed out implausibilities in the story. 'Do you know what I'd do,' he said as Dorothy forced Jeffrey to undress at knife-point. 'I'd grab the knife off her. This is a serious point. It's not a very convincing confrontation.' He found Frank genuinely disturbing, but it bothered him that Jeffrey should be able to turn up at Dorothy's apartment several times without anyone apparently noticing, since earlier we are told that the police have been keeping the building under surveillance. 'The other thing – Dorothy gets beaten around all the time, but she's got no bruises.' In the finale, when Jeffrey tricks Frank into hunting for him in the back bedroom, he couldn't understand why he then chose to hide in Dorothy's **closet** again: 'I'd get the hell out of there.'

The story for him was the film's great failing: 'It just doesn't make sense. You could write the script in a number of different ways and it wouldn't make any difference. As you wait for the plot to thicken and develop, you're very aware that it's not a story that will logically unfold. It's unpredictable and you have no idea where it's going. It just takes its own course.'

We talked about the characters. Jeffrey he thought was 'a bit mad really'. Frank was a 'great guy', he joked. 'He's a megalomaniac. He likes to dominate. I wouldn't say he's evil. He's just mad. How much that's through **drug** abuse, it's difficult to say, but he's a bad egg.' And Dorothy? 'Pathetic. Pathetic. Just basically one of life's victims.' The only character he felt was at all believable was Sandy. Generally, he thought the characters were undeveloped: 'The things they do, the lives they lead – people don't lead lives like that. All you see are their dark sides.'

He didn't really like the film. Not that he thought it was bad; it was just weird. He could appreciate that it operated according to different rules from what he would more normally go and see. But they weren't rules he had any time for. He found it peculiar that anyone should want to linger on degradation. This seems to me to be the fundamental reason why so many people react strongly against David Lynch's films. It's a basic human need to to look upon life as an essentially pleasurable and fulfilling experience. Even the most violent mainstream Hollywood films obey this rule. For with their heroes and villains outlook and their tightly plotted stories, they imply a world of order, from which the **darkness** they depict is a departure. But *Blue Velvet* suggests that such darkness is an innate part of what we consider to be our ordered world.

A few days later I was watching the Saturday-night movie on TV. It happened to be *The Hand that Rocks the Cradle*, but it could have been *Malice* or *Pacific Heights* or, with very few exceptions, any of the other thrillers to have rolled off the conveyor belt of the Hollywood studios in recent years. Hugely professional, hugely impressive. The **plot**, with all its intricacies, is likely a finely built car. You can't help but admire the way everything hangs together, and the way it gears you up, so that as the finale approaches your heart is in your mouth.

But, although a lot will happen, somehow there's nothing to find out. The characters are types whose part in the drama we recognise instantly. The middle-class couple, with their newborn child, living in a huge clapboard house; the nanny seeking revenge; the misunderstood simpleton, who we somehow know from our first sight of him will come to the rescue in the end; the family friend who sees through the nanny's deceit. At the end of the film the characters remain somehow unchanged by what they've been through; you feel they can just slot back into their previous lives as if nothing had happened at all, just as we, the audience, can leave the cinema or turn off the TV and pretty much have forgotten the film by the next morning.

There's plenty of action in the showdown, as the family discover who the murderous nanny is, but it's a series of ever-increasing bursts like the end of a firework show – no single incident is dwelt on in any detail. There is no **texture**. Everything is flat, everything is subordinated to the dynamo of the plot, including truth and character. But maybe this is the nature of contemporary life. People take their meals and their entertainment on the run.

W

Williams, Detective

Detective Williams believes in a clear division between the world of adults and the world of **children**. When Jeffrey brings him the severed **ear** he asks him not to tell anyone and not even to ask about the case. As far as Detective Williams is concerned, this is no longer Jeffrey's business. When later Jeffrey brings him some more evidence of what Frank and his **gang** are up to, including the information that there is a traitor in the Police Department, he's more cross than grateful. Jeffrey has been meddling in dangerous matters best left to the grown-ups.

There's a stark division in the film between the responsible and irresponsible adults. While the latter whoop it up, the former are steady, sober, even rather subdued figures. It's as if they have too many of the cares of the world on their shoulders to be cheerful. Detective Williams tells Jeffrey that it was curiosity that got him into the detective business, but if so it has long since dried up, and he seems far more aware of the grim aspects of his job. Jeffrey says that being a detective 'must be great', but Detective Williams points out that 'it's horrible too'. When Jeffrey shows him the severed ear, he treats it as an unremarkable, routine discovery: 'It's an ear, all right.' He's seen too much to be surprised by anything.

Being grown-up is about controlling your feelings and keeping things hidden. When Jeffrey meets the police traitor Detective Gordon (the Yellow Man) in Sandy's house he's so shocked that Detective

Williams has to intervene with some 'fatherly advice' to stop him from saying anything.

He is a man who wears his gun in his living room, pinned to his chest in a shoulder holster. He seems imprisoned by the thing, his natural stance one of vigilance and suspicion. He has no life outside his duty as a policeman and as a responsible parent.

See **Dickerson, George**.

Williams, Mrs

Like Mrs Beaumont, Sandy's mother is a shadowy figure. But while Mrs Beaumont seldom raises herself from her sofa, Mrs Williams does make herself a little bit more useful. She's the dramatic equivalent of a spear carrier in a Greek tragedy. Support and helpmeet, she's there to open the door to Jeffrey, fix her daughter's dress and summon ambulances.

See **Lange, Hope**.

Williams, Sandy

See **Sandy**.

Wilmington

The city in North Carolina where *Blue Velvet* was made. Shooting took place there to take advantage of De Laurentiis Entertainment Group's new studios, which had just been built. The name Lynch chose for his fictional town was **Lumberton**. The production designer **Patty Norris** had told him that if he picked a town somewhere in North Carolina the police would let them use their insignia for free: 'So I looked at the map and bingo! Lumberton leaped out like a frog.' It was this choice of name which then inspired Lynch to imagine the setting of *Blue Velvet* as the sort of logging town that he would have known as a child.

The particular Lumberton he chose was about seventy miles to the north-west of Wilmington. As accidental as it may have been, it's in keeping with the **dualist** vision of *Blue Velvet* that the Lumberton we see on the screen should be called by one town's name but really be another.

The nostalgic visions of forests and logs aside, this town isn't meant to be anywhere in particular – it's Anyplace, USA – but, for the record, the river we see briefly in the film is the Cape Fear. Lynch's next feature film, *Wild at Heart*, would open with this title: 'Cape Fear, somewhere near the border between North and South Carolina.'

Wizard of Oz, The

David Lynch does not so much allude to the 1939 Judy Garland film as draw on something that has become part of the fabric of **American** life. Its importance to *Blue Velvet* is such that it's worth giving a brief summary.

When Dorothy Gale's dog Toto bites Miss Gulch, the wicked old lady threatens to have the dog taken away and destroyed. Dorothy is distraught and rushes home to tell her aunt and uncle. But they have a crisis to attend to on their farm and have no time to listen to her problems. 'Find yourself a place where there isn't any trouble,' says Aunt Em, who wants to get her out from under her feet.

'A place where there isn't any trouble,' muses Dorothy wistfully. Such a place can only exist somewhere over the rainbow. And she sings the song.

Miss Gulch gets a warrant from the Sherriff and duly takes Toto away, but the dog escapes and returns to Dorothy. Afraid that Miss Gulch will soon be back, Dorothy and Toto run away. Dorothy meets a fortune teller who persuades her to go back home, but then a tornado whisks her off to the Land of Oz. Here the Good Witch tells her to see the Wizard, who will be able to advise her how to get home, and she sets off along the Yellow Brick Road, to be joined along the way by the Scarecrow, the Tin Man and the Cowardly Lion.

Blue Velvet and *The Wizard of Oz* – if any cinema would dare such a thing – would make the perfect double bill. Both are **fairy tales** which deal with the same things – the getting of wisdom and the struggle between good and evil. *The Wizard of Oz* so captured Lynch's imagination that *Blue Velvet* can seem like a variation on a theme.

Dorothy Vallens, like her namesake, wears red shoes. Frank imprisons Dorothy Vallens' little boy Donny, just as the Wicked Witch tries to kidnap Dorothy Gale's dog. One of Donny's toys, which Jeffrey discovers in his mother's apartment, is a little wizard's hat with a propeller on top. At the end of the film, when mother and son are reunited, we see Donny wearing it. Lynch was delighted to discover that Dennis Hopper came from Kansas, and doubtless would have regarded it as another pleasing coincidence that Hopper's character Frank Booth shares a Christian name with the actor Frank Morgan, who plays the Wizard of Oz and his counterpart in Kansas, Professor Marvel. Just as the professor adopts several disguises (as well as the Wizard, he's also a doorkeeper, a soldier and a cabby in Emerald City), Frank has his disguise as the well-dressed man.

As significant as these direct correspondences is a shared feel for texture and sensibility. The red roses and yellow tulips in the opening sequence of *Blue Velvet*, unearthly in their brilliance, could easily have been plucked in the rich Technicolor Land of Oz. The Haunted Forest, with its mechanical owls, the stylised decor of the Witch's Castle and Emerald City, the stark contrast between light and dark, the use of **music** to articulate mood – all these things would have appealed to Lynch.

Dorothy Gale in *The Wizard of Oz* may lack a little self-confidence, but she proves to be brave and self-reliant. In spite of being frightened, she slaps the Lion on the nose when he attacks her dog Toto. 'Shame on you!' she cries. 'It's bad enough picking on a Straw Man but when you go around picking on poor little dogs . . .' Whatever Dorothy Gale's troubles may be, she has continued to follow the Yellow Brick Road and we feel that she is well on the way to finding an answer.

But Dorothy Vallens is hopelessly lost in the forest, where she has tumbled into a deep abyss. **Deep River Apartments** is where she lives, and she's drowning. Her helplessness is all the more poignant because she is no longer a **child**, like Dorothy Gale, but a grown woman. Her troubles make those of her counterpart in *The Wizard of Oz* seem slight by comparison.

While *The Wizard of Oz* was made by a team of professional optimists, *Blue Velvet* was the personal vision of an artist as determined to examine the unpleasant side of life as MGM was to bury it. But Judy Garland, one feels, would have recognised **the Blue Lady**, a singer like herself. For awaiting MGM's icon of innocence – further along the Yellow Brick Road – was a life of depression and pills and repeated suicide attempts. In Lynch's script, but not the finished film, there was a scene in which Dorothy took Jeffrey up on to the roof of Deep River Apartments. As the tune of 'Somewhere Over the Rainbow' plays in the background, she shows him where she intends to throw herself off and end it all.

But Lynch finds a beauty in things which in *The Wizard of Oz* are only to be feared. As Dorothy Gale and her companions leave the dark forest behind and stride confidently towards Emerald City, joyful voices sing: 'You're out of the woods, you're out of the dark, you're out of the night.' In *Blue Velvet* the **darkness** and the night are depicted as mysterious and dangerous but also as attractive for the **secrets** that they hide. Jeffrey willingly journeys into the darkness as he seeks to unravel the mystery of the severed **ear**, and it is from out of the darkness that the angelic Sandy first emerges.

I have in front of me the *Official 50th Anniversary Pictorial History* of the film. In a chapter called 'Icons', it lists the many movie allusions to the film, from *Flash Gordon* to *Who Framed Roger Rabbit?* But no mention is made of *Blue Velvet*, even although its relationship with *The Wizard of Oz* is one of the most profound. With a fan's devotion, Lynch would return to *The Wizard of Oz* in his next feature film, *Wild at Heart*, where the references were even more overt.

Y

Yellow Man, the

The Yellow Man, otherwise known as Detective T. R. Gordon, is in secret working for Frank's **gang**, arresting **drug** dealers and passing their merchandise on to the criminals. He wears a yellow suit, which perhaps ought to have at least aroused the **Lumberton** Police Department's suspicions. The colour is an age-old symbol of treachery. In medieval paintings Judas is always dressed in it.

In the film the Yellow Man scarcely says a word, and we have no idea how he became a traitor. But Lynch cut out a scene in the script which both explained this and provided some background detail about Dorothy's husband. The Yellow Man drops by Dorothy's apartment looking for sexual favours. Dorothy turns him away by telling him that soon Frank's going to arrive:

YELLOW MAN: He's comin' back? What for?

DOROTHY: 'Cause he's comin' back, that's what for. Frank's got you really loaded tonight.

YELLOW MAN: Yeah, maybe so. Frank's got me. And you. And really it's all thanks to Don, isn't it? Remember that. Your husband was the one who started fucking my mind with drugs.

DOROTHY: Oh, he forced you, huh?

YELLOW MAN: Remember, he's the reformed dealer who wanted to turn himself in. He's the one that caused Frank to come, and Frank's

fucking us real good. I just feel so horny. I'm supposed to be here
watching you. Why can't I be here fucking you, too. Listen. I know
his cock's the size of a pin – let me give you the real thing. Let me
wet my whistle, baby.

Dorothy threatens to tell Frank what the Yellow Man has said, and he
leaves the apartment.

The scene contains little information that we really need or can't
guess for ourselves. It exists only to explain things, with no inner life
of its own. The Yellow Man is just one character too many, and his
sexual obsession with Dorothy would have undermined the dramatic
focus of the ménage à trois between Dorothy, Jeffrey and Frank.

By revealing that Dorothy's husband Don was a drug dealer, the scene
makes Dorothy appear less a victim and more a part of Frank's world.
She loses her mystery. In the finished film the pathos of Dorothy is that
her suffering comes from nowhere, and she seems like a stranger lost in
an alien land.

Z

Zippergate

Perhaps the whole idea of the **American** dream makes a sharp contrast between façade and reality an inevitable part of national life. The American people have been forged in the conviction that life can be perfect.

This goes to the very top. I am writing these words in the days of Zippergate. Monica Lewinsky's blue dress has been taken away for DNA sampling, jokes about her assignations with the President abound (Why is there no proof? She swallowed the evidence.) and every day there are more stories about the Good Bill and the Bad Bill.

There are countless versions of the truth, but what is most obvious is the readiness of a people to delude itself in order to believe in the irreproachability of the President of the United States. They want only to see the immaculate green lawn, and to forget the bugs beneath – which is fair enough.

Sources

Sources

Note: All references to the script of *Blue Velvet* are to the Revised Third Draft, dated 24 July 1985, a copy of which is held by the British Film Institute Library.

Bacon

'and it was . . .': Chris Rodley (ed.), *Lynch on Lynch* (Faber & Faber, 1997), p.16.

'suddenly fear like . . .', 'The noise of . . .' and 'uncalled for and . . .': introduction, *Bacon: Portraits and Self-Portraits* (Thames & Hudson, 1997).

Connections

'photographs of people . . .' and 'every piece of . . .': *Hitchcock on Hitchcock* (Faber, 1995), p.290.

Laura Dern

'I chose to . . .': *Sunday Telegraph Magazine*, 26 August 1990.

Dorothy

'cows hanging in . . .': *Interview*, April 1988.

'When I was . . .': *Village Voice*, 23 September 1986.

Duality, double identity and doubles
'something out of . . .': ibid.

The Duck
'How a duck . . .': *Rolling Stone*, 6 September 1990.

The Ear
'It had to . . .': *Lynch on Lynch*, p.136.

Elmes, Frederick
'Both evoke very . . .': *American Cinematographer*, October 1989.
'By not explaining . . .': ibid.

Families
'This is the . . .': *Moving Pictures*, BBC TV, 1992.

Frank
'Frank . . . well, he . . .': *The Face*, August 1987.

Genre
'I love 47 . . .': *Time*, 1 October 1990.

Henri, Robert
'It became . . . my . . .':*Lynch on Lynch*, p.9.
'The great artist . . .' and 'Low art is . . .': Quoted in Gail Levin,
    Edward Hopper (W.W. Norton & Co, 1980), p.20.

Hopper, Dennis
'It wasn't so . . .': Quoted in *Life Magazine, Observer*, 18 September
    1994.
'You gotta do . . .': *Interview*, October 1994, p.148.

'Since *Blue Velvet* . . .': *The Face*, August 1987.

Hopper, Edward
'You must not . . .': Quoted in Gail Levin, *Edward Hopper*, p.45.

Influences
'An anomaly – the . . .': Paulin Kael, *The New Yorker*, September 1986.

Lynch, David
'My father . . . would . . .': *Time*, 1 October 1990.
'I feel between . . .': *Lynch on Lynch*, p.14.
'Once you have . . .': *Rolling Stone*, 6 September 1990.
'elegant homes, tree-lined . . .': *Lynch on Lynch*, p.10.
'Going into the . . .' and 'It was the . . .': *Rolling Stone*, 6 September 1990.
'I could just . . .': *Lynch on Lynch*, p.8.
'The things that . . .': ibid, p.32.
'a super-cool thing . . .': *Interview*, March 1987.
'I never wanted . . .': *Lynch on Lynch*, p.37.
'It was a . . .': ibid, p.38.
'I lived on . . .': *Rolling Stone*, 6 September 1990.
'I like to . . .': *Süddeutsche Zeitung*, September 1990.
'little by little . . .': *Lynch on Lynch*, p.120.
'I was making . . .': *Time*, 10 January 1990.
'It's an American . . .': *Interview*, March 1987.
'Lynch learned a . . .': *American Cinematographer*, November 1986.

MacLachlan, Kyle
'I'm a pretty . . .': *Daily Mail*, 16 February 1991

'MacLachlan seems to . . .': ibid, 16 February 1991.
'No, not at . . .': *Empire*, January 1998.

Mood
'It is in . . .': *De Profundis*.

Music
'You rarely get . . .': *Lynch on Lynch*, p.127.
'A song to . . .': ibid, p.132.
'David does not . . .': *Kinorevue*, October 1996.
'like the rich . . .': Michael Powell, *A Life in Movies* (Heinemann, 1986), p.582.

Nance, Jack
'was a pretty . . .': *Starlog*, 1990.
'a fairly strange . . .': *Premiere*, August 1997.
'I always say . . .': *Starlog*, 1990.

Norris, Patricia
'Patty created the . . .': *American Cintematographer*, March 1987.
'I collaborate with . . .': *Pretty as a Picture: The Art of David Lynch* (US 1997), directed by Toby Keeler.
'All rooms come . . .': *American Cinematographer*, March 1987.

Philadelphia
'All that protected . . .': *Lynch on Lynch*, p.43.

Providence
'The dream gave . . .': *Lynch on Lynch*, p.136.
'If you're quiet . . .': *Marie Claire*, February 1997.
'explained to me . . .': *Lynch on Lynch*, p.128.
'There was the . . .': ibid, p.128.

'He turned it . . .': ibid, p.128.
'A film exists . . .': *Rolling Stone*, 6 March 1997.

Rossellini, Isabella
'You could . . .' and 'You idiot . . .': *New York Times*, 11 October 1986.

Sex
'it can be . . .': *Film Comment*, September/October 1986.
'the vast realm . . .': *Rolling Stone*, 6 September 1990.
'It's the key . . .': ibid.

Shostakovitch
'Make it with . . .': *Millimeter*, November 1986.

The Sickest Film Ever Made?
'What Lynch shows . . .': Geoff Andrew, *Time Out*, March 4–11, 1987.
'The view of . . .': *New Statesman*, 10 April 1987.
'It's harrowing stuff . . .': *Today*, 10 April 1987.
'*Blue Velvet* is . . .': *Morning Star*, 10 April 1987.
'This is an . . .': Barry Gifford, *The Devil Thumbs a Ride and Other Unforgettable Films* (Grove Press, New York, 1988).

Sound
'He's definitely not . . .': *Mix Magazine*, January 1997.

Splet, Alan R.
'The trick is . . .': *Millimeter*, November 1986.
'we hit a . . .': ibid.
'Then we turned . . .': ibid.
'when you have . . .': *Lynch on Lynch*, p.129.

Stockwell, Dean
'flamboyant, debonair, quality . . .': *Married to the Mob* publicity
  release, Dean Stockwell microfiche, BFI Library.

'This is It'
'too much of . . .': *Lynch on Lynch*, p.146.

Twelve Years On
'I really believe . . .': *Film Comment*, September/October 1987.

Voyeurism
'I told him . . .': *Lynch on Lynch*, pp.135–6.

Wilmington
'So I looked . . .': *Interview*, March 1987.

Charles Drazin was born in Farnborough, Hampshire, in 1960. He was educated at Highgate School and Oxford, and has worked as an editor in publishing. He has contributed to several newspapers and magazines. His first book *The Finest Years* was published in 1998.